SECRETS
OF THE
UNIVERSE

SECRETS

OF THE

UNIVERSE

Scenes from the Journey Home

SCOTT RUSSELL SANDERS

BEACON PRESS
BOSTON

Beacon Press
25 Beacon Street
Boston, Massachusetts 02108

Beacon Press books
are published under the auspices of
the Unitarian Universalist Association of Congregations.

98 97   8 7 6 5 4 3

Text design by Ruth Kolbert

Earlier versions of these essays appeared in the following publica-
tions: "Under the Influence" in Harper's Magazine, "Reasons of the
Body" in The Georgia Review, "Looking at Women" in The Georgia
Review, "Dust" in The Kenyon Review, "Landscape and Imagina-
tion" in The North American Review, "Local Matters" in Wigwag,
"Signs" in The North American Review, "Grub" in Wigwag, "Yard
Birds" in The North American Review, "Jailhouse Blues" in The
North American Review, "Living Souls" in The Georgia Review, "The
Singular First Person" in Sewanee Review, "Speaking a Word for
Nature" in Michigan Quarterly Review, "Tokens of Mystery" in
Orion Nature Quarterly, "Secrets of the Universe" in The North
American Review. "Talking Dust Bowl," words and music by Woody
Guthrie, TRO © 1961, renewed by Ludlow Music, Inc., New
York, and "Star Dust," words by Mitchell Parish and music by
Hoagy Carmichael, © 1929 (renewed 1957) by Mills Music, Inc.,
all rights reserved, used by permission.

Library of Congress Cataloging-in-Publication Data

Sanders, Scott R. (Scott Russell), 1945–
Secrets of the universe: scenes from the journey home /
Scott Russell Sanders.
p.   cm.
ISBN 0-8070-6330-4 (cloth)
ISBN 0-8070-6331-2 (paper)
I. Title.
PS3569.A5137S4   1991
814'.54—dc20   91-10219

FOR
William and Martha Schafer,
who speak to my condition

CONTENTS

PREFACE

Often I wake in the night, feeling panicky, not knowing where I am. I reach out to stroke my wife's shoulder. I peer into the dark, searching for the moonlit rectangle of a window, the lacy outline of a fern on the sill. I listen for the creak of old timbers in the house, the sound of my children's breathing, the drowsy chatter of birds. In the night, as in the day, I locate myself through what I love.

What I love binds me in cords that stretch to infinity. In these essays I begin with the fierce, tangled relations between parent and child, between man and woman. From the family I move to the larger loyalties of neighborhood, community, and region. Then I speak of belonging to nature, this order that sustains us,

and of inhabiting the earth. Finally, warily, I reflect on
that encompassing mystery we call the universe. The
movement outward to greater and greater circles is also
a movement inward, ever closer to the center from
which creation springs.

I do not expect to arrive at the absolute center or
circumference of things, at least not along a path of
words. I will follow that path as far as it leads, then go
on ahead in silence. The journey home is my effort to
come fully awake, to understand where I actually live.
If, on the way, I have discovered any secrets worth telling, they must be ones known to all of us in our clear
moments. I seek a truth as common as dirt or laughter,
and as rare.

The most beautiful thing we can experience is the
mysterious.
It is the source of all true art and science.

—ALBERT EINSTEIN

I

PEOPLE

UNDER

THE

INFLUENCE

MY FATHER DRANK. HE DRANK AS A GUT-PUNCHED
boxer gasps for breath, as a starving dog gobbles food—
compulsively, secretly, in pain and trembling. I use the
past tense not because he ever quit drinking but because
he quit living. That is how the story ends for my father,
age sixty-four, heart bursting, body cooling and forsaken
on the linoleum of my brother's trailer. The story continues for my brother, my sister, my mother, and me,
and will continue so long as memory holds.

In the perennial present of memory, I slip into the
garage or barn to see my father tipping back the flat
green bottles of wine, the brown cylinders of whiskey,
the cans of beer disguised in paper bags. His Adam's ap-
ple bobs, the liquid gurgles, he wipes the sandy-haired

back of a hand over his lips, and then, his bloodshot gaze bumping into me, he stashes the bottle or can inside his jacket, under the workbench, between two bales of hay, and we both pretend the moment has not occurred.

"What's up, buddy?" he says, thick-tongued and edgy.

"Sky's up," I answer, playing along.

"And don't forget prices," he grumbles. "Prices are always up. And taxes."

In memory, his white 1951 Pontiac with the stripes down the hood and the Indian head on the snout jounces to a stop in the driveway; or it is the 1956 Ford station wagon, or the 1963 Rambler shaped like a toad, or the sleek 1969 Bonneville that will do 120 miles per hour on straightaways; or it is the robin's-egg blue pickup, new in 1980, battered in 1981, the year of his death. He climbs out, grinning dangerously, unsteady on his legs, and we children interrupt our game of catch, our building of snow forts, our picking of plums, to watch in silence as he weaves past into the house, where he slumps into his overstuffed chair and falls asleep. Shaking her head, our mother stubs out the cigarette he has left smoldering in the ashtray. All evening, until our bedtimes, we tiptoe past him, as past a snoring dragon. Then we curl in our fearful sheets, listening. Eventually he wakes with a grunt, Mother slings accusations at him, he snarls back, she yells, he growls, their voices clashing. Before long, she retreats to their bedroom, sobbing—not from the blows of fists, for he never strikes her, but from the force of words.

Left alone, our father prowls the house, thumping into furniture, rummaging in the kitchen, slamming doors, turning the pages of the newspaper with a savage crackle, muttering back at the late-night drivel from television. The roof might fly off, the walls might buckle from the pressure of his rage. Whatever my brother and sister and mother may be thinking on their own rumpled pillows, I lie there hating him, loving him, fearing him, knowing I have failed him. I tell myself he drinks to ease an ache that gnaws at his belly, an ache I must have caused by disappointing him somehow, a murderous ache I should be able to relieve by doing all my chores, earning A's in school, winning baseball games, fixing the broken washer and the burst pipes, bringing in money to fill his empty wallet. He would not hide the green bottles in his tool box, would not sneak off to the barn with a lump under his coat, would not fall asleep in the daylight, would not roar and fume, would not drink himself to death, if only I were perfect.

I am forty-two as I write these words, and I know full well now that my father was an alcoholic, a man consumed by disease rather than by disappointment. What had seemed to me a private grief is in fact a public scourge. In the United States alone some ten or fifteen million people share his ailment, and behind the doors they slam in fury or disgrace, countless other children tremble. I comfort myself with such knowledge, holding it against the throb of memory like an ice pack against a bruise. There are keener sources of grief: poverty, racism, rape, war. I do not wish to compete for a trophy in suffering. I am only trying to understand the corrosive mixture of helplessness, responsibility, and shame that I learned to feel as the son of an alcoholic. I realize now that I did not cause my father's illness, nor could I have cured it. Yet for all this grown-up knowledge, I am still ten years old, my own son's age, and as that boy I struggle in guilt and confusion to save my father from pain.

CONSIDER A FEW of our synonyms for *drunk:* tipsy, tight, pickled, soused, and plowed; stoned and stewed, lubricated and inebriated, juiced and sluiced; three sheets to the wind, in your cups, out of your mind, under the table; lit up, tanked up, wiped out; besotted, blotto, bombed, and buzzed; plastered, polluted, putrified; loaded or looped, boozy, woozy, fuddled, or smashed; crocked and shit-faced, corked and pissed, snockered and sloshed.

It is a mostly humorous lexicon, as the lore that deals with drunks—in jokes and cartoons, in plays, films, and television skits—is largely comic. Aunt Matilda nips elderberry wine from the sideboard and burps politely during supper. Uncle Fred slouches to the table glassy-eyed, wearing a lamp shade for a hat and murmuring, "Candy is dandy but liquor is quicker." Inspired by cocktails, Mrs. Somebody recounts the events of her day in a fuzzy dialect, while Mr. Somebody nibbles her ear and croons a bawdy song. On the sofa with Boyfriend, Daughter giggles, licking gin from her lips, and loosens the bows in her hair. Junior knocks back some brews with his chums at the Leopard Lounge and stumbles home to the wrong house, wonders foggily why he cannot locate his pajamas, and crawls naked into bed with the ugliest girl in school. The family dog slurps from a neglected martini and wobbles to the nursery, where he vomits in Baby's shoe.

It is all great fun. But if in the audience you notice

a few laughing faces turn grim when the drunk lurches on stage, don't be surprised, for these are the children of alcoholics. Over the grinning mask of Dionysus, the leering mask of Bacchus, these children cannot help seeing the bloated features of their own parents. Instead of laughing, they wince, they mourn. Instead of celebrating the drunk as one freed from constraints, they pity him as one enslaved. They refuse to believe in *vino veritas*, having seen their befuddled parents skid away from truth toward folly and oblivion. And so these children bite their lips until the lush staggers into the wings.

My father, when drunk, was neither funny nor honest; he was pathetic, frightening, deceitful. There seemed to be a leak in him somewhere, and he poured in booze to keep from draining dry. Like a torture victim who refuses to squeal, he would never admit that he had touched a drop, not even in his last year, when he seemed to be dissolving in alcohol before our very eyes. I never knew him to lie about anything, ever, except about this one ruinous fact. Drowsy, clumsy, unable to fix a bicycle tire, throw a baseball, balance a grocery sack, or walk across the room, he was stripped of his true self by drink. In a matter of minutes, the contents of a bottle could transform a brave man into a coward, a buddy into a bully, a gifted athlete and skilled carpenter and shrewd businessman into a bumbler. No dictionary of synonyms for *drunk* would soften the anguish of watching our prince turn into a frog.

FATHER'S DRINKING became the family secret. While growing up, we children never breathed a word of it beyond the four walls of our house. To this day, my brother and sister rarely mention it, and then only when I press them. I did not confess the ugly, bewildering fact to my wife until his wavering walk and slurred speech forced me to. Recently, on the seventh anniversary of my father's death, I asked my mother if she ever spoke of his drinking to friends. "No, no, never," she replied hastily. "I couldn't bear for anyone to know."

The secret bores under the skin, gets in the blood, into the bone, and stays there. Long after you have supposedly been cured of malaria, the fever can flare up, the tremors can shake you. So it is with the fevers of shame. You swallow the bitter quinine of knowledge, and you learn to feel pity and compassion toward the drinker. Yet the shame lingers in your marrow, and, because of the shame, anger.

FOR A LONG STRETCH of my childhood we lived on a military reservation in Ohio, an arsenal where bombs were stored underground in bunkers, vintage airplanes burst into flames, and unstable artillery shells boomed nightly at the dump. We had the feeling, as children, that we played in a mine field, where a heedless footfall could trigger an explosion. When Father was drinking, the house, too, became a mine field. The least bump could set off either parent.

The more he drank, the more obsessed Mother became with stopping him. She hunted for bottles, counted the cash in his wallet, sniffed at his breath. Without meaning to snoop, we children blundered left and right into damning evidence. On afternoons when he came home from work sober, we flung ourselves at him for hugs, and felt against our ribs the telltale lump in his coat. In the barn we tumbled on the hay and heard beneath our sneakers the crunch of buried glass. We tugged open a drawer in his workbench, looking for screwdrivers or crescent wrenches, and spied a gleaming six-pack among the tools. Playing tag, we darted around the house just in time to see him sway on the rear stoop and heave a finished bottle into the woods. In his good night kiss we smelled the cloying sweetness of Clorets, the mints he chewed to camouflage his dragon's breath.

I can summon up that kiss right now by recalling Theodore Roethke's lines about his own father in "My Papa's Waltz":

> The whiskey on your breath
> Could make a small boy dizzy;
> But I hung on like death:
> Such waltzing was not easy.

Such waltzing was hard, terribly hard, for with a boy's scrawny arms I was trying to hold my tipsy father upright.

For years, the chief source of those incriminating bottles and cans was a grimy store a mile from us, a cinder block place called Sly's, with two gas pumps outside and a moth-eaten dog asleep in the window. A strip of flypaper, speckled the year round with black bodies, coiled in the doorway. Inside, on rusty metal shelves or in wheezing coolers, you could find pop and Popsicles, cigarettes, potato chips, canned soup, raunchy postcards, fishing gear, Twinkies, wine, and beer. When Fa-

9

ther drove anywhere on errands, Mother would send us kids along as guards, warning us not to let him out of our sight. And so with one or more of us on board, Father would cruise up to Sly's, pump a dollar's worth of gas or plump the tires with air, and then, telling us to wait in the car, he would head for that fly-spangled doorway.

Dutiful and panicky, we cried, "Let us go in with you!"

"No," he answered. "I'll be back in two shakes."

"Please!"

"No!" he roared. "Don't you budge, or I'll jerk a knot in your tails!"

So we stayed put, kicking the seats, while he ducked inside. Often, when he had parked the car at a careless angle, we gazed in through the window and saw Mr. Sly fetching down from a shelf behind the cash register two green pints of Gallo wine. Father swigged one of them right there at the counter, stuffed the other in his pocket, and then out he came, a bulge in his coat, a flustered look on his red face.

Because the Mom and Pop who ran the dump were neighbors of ours, living just down the tar-blistered road, I hated them all the more for poisoning my father. I wanted to sneak in their store and smash the bottles and set fire to the place. I also hated the Gallo brothers, Ernest and Julio, whose jovial faces shone from the labels of their wine, labels I would find, torn and curled, when I burned the trash. I noted the Gallo brothers' address, in California, and I studied the road atlas to see how far that was from Ohio, because I meant to go out there and tell Ernest and Julio what they were doing to my father, and then, if they showed no mercy, I would kill them.

WHILE GROWING UP on the back roads and in the country schools and cramped Methodist churches of Ohio and Tennessee, I never heard the word *alcoholism*, never happened across it in books or magazines. In the nearby towns, there were no addiction treatment programs, no community mental health centers, no Alcoholics Anonymous chapters, no therapists. Left alone with our grievous secret, we had no way of understanding Father's drinking except as an act of will, a deliberate folly or cruelty, a moral weakness, a sin. He drank because he chose to, pure and simple. Why our father, so playful and competent and kind when sober, would choose to ruin himself and punish his family, we could not fathom.

Our neighborhood was high on the Bible, and the Bible was hard on drunkards. "Woe to those who are heroes at drinking wine, and valiant men in mixing strong drink," wrote Isaiah. "The priest and the prophet reel with strong drink, they are confused with wine, they err in vision, they stumble in giving judgment. For all tables are full of vomit, no place is without filthiness." We children had seen those fouled tables at the local truck stop where the notorious boozers hung out, our father occasionally among them. "Wine and new wine take away the understanding," declared the prophet Hosea. We had also seen evidence of that in our father, who could multiply seven-digit numbers in his head when sober, but when drunk could not help us with fourth-grade math. Proverbs warned: "Do not look at wine when it is red, when it sparkles in the cup and goes down smoothly. At the last it bites like a serpent, and stings like an adder. Your eyes will see strange things, and your mind utter perverse things." Woe, woe.

Dismayingly often, these biblical drunkards stirred up trouble for their own kids. Noah made fresh wine after the flood, drank too much of it, fell asleep without any clothes on, and was glimpsed in the buff by his son Ham, whom Noah promptly cursed. In one passage—it was so shocking we had to read it under our blankets with flashlights—the patriarch Lot fell down drunk and slept with his daughters. The sins of the fathers set their children's teeth on edge.

Our ministers were fond of quoting St. Paul's pronouncement that drunkards would not inherit the kingdom of God. These grave preachers assured us that the wine referred to during the Last Supper was in fact grape juice. Bible and sermons and hymns combined to give us the impression that Moses should have brought down from the mountain another stone tablet, bearing the Eleventh Commandment: Thou shalt not drink.

The scariest and most illuminating Bible story apropos of drunkards was the one about the lunatic and the swine. Matthew, Mark, and Luke each told a version of the tale. We knew it by heart: When Jesus climbed out of his boat one day, this lunatic came charging up from the graveyard, stark naked and filthy, frothing at the mouth, so violent that he broke the strongest chains. Nobody would go near him. Night and day for years this madman had been wailing among the tombs and bruising himself with stones. Jesus took one look at him and said,

"Come out of the man, you unclean spirits!" for he could see that the lunatic was possessed by demons. Meanwhile, some hogs were conveniently rooting nearby. "If we have to come out," begged the demons, "at least let us go into those swine." Jesus agreed. The unclean spirits entered the hogs, and the hogs rushed straight off a cliff and plunged into a lake. Hearing the story in Sunday school, my friends thought mainly of the pigs. (How big a splash did they make? Who paid for the lost pork?) But I thought of the redeemed lunatic, who bathed himself and put on clothes and calmly sat at the feet of Jesus, restored—so the Bible said—to "his right mind."

When drunk, our father was clearly in his wrong mind. He became a stranger, as fearful to us as any graveyard lunatic, not quite frothing at the mouth but fierce enough, quick-tempered, explosive; or else he grew maudlin and weepy, which frightened us nearly as much. In my boyhood despair, I reasoned that maybe he wasn't to blame for turning into an ogre. Maybe, like the lunatic, he was possessed by demons. I found support for my theory when I heard liquor referred to as "spirits," when the newspapers reported that somebody had been arrested for "driving under the influence," and when church ladies railed against that "demon drink."

If my father was indeed possessed, who would exorcise him? If he was a sinner, who would save him? If he was ill, who would cure him? If he suffered, who would ease his pain? Not ministers or doctors, for we could not bring ourselves to confide in them; not the neighbors, for we pretended they had never seen him drunk; not Mother, who fussed and pleaded but could not budge him; not my brother and sister, who were only kids. That left me. It did not matter that I, too, was only a child, and a bewildered one at that. I could not excuse myself.

ON FIRST READING a description of delirium tremens—in a book on alcoholism I smuggled from the library—I thought immediately of the frothing lunatic and the frenzied swine. When I read stories or watched films about grisly metamorphoses—Dr. Jekyll becoming Mr. Hyde, the mild husband changing into a werewolf, the kindly neighbor taken over by a brutal alien—I could not help seeing my own father's mutation from sober to drunk. Even today, knowing better, I am attracted by the demonic theory of drink, for when I recall my father's transformation, the emergence of his ugly second self, I find it easy to believe in possession by unclean spirits. We never knew which version of Father would come home from work, the true or the tainted, nor could we guess how far down the slope toward cruelty he would slide.

How far a man *could* slide we gauged by observing our back-road neighbors—the out-of-work miners who had dragged their families to our corner of Ohio from the desolate hollows of Appalachia, the tightfisted farmers, the surly mechanics, the balked and broken men. There was, for example, whiskey-soaked Mr. Jenkins, who beat his wife and kids so hard we could hear their screams from the road. There was Mr. Lavo the wino, who fell asleep smoking time and again, until one night his disgusted wife bundled up the children and went outside and left him in his easy chair to burn; he awoke on his own, staggered out coughing into the yard, and pounded her flat while the children looked on and the shack turned to ash. There was the truck driver, Mr. Sampson, who tripped over his son's tricycle one night while drunk and got so mad that he jumped into his semi and drove away, shifting through the dozen gears, and never came back. We saw the bruised children of these fathers clump onto our school bus, we saw the abandoned children huddle in the pews at church, we saw the stunned and battered mothers begging for help at our doors.

Our own father never beat us, and I don't think he ever beat Mother, but he threatened often. The Old Testament Yahweh was not more terrible in his wrath. Eyes blazing, voice booming, Father would pull out his belt and swear to give us a whipping, but he never followed through, never needed to, because we could imagine it so vividly. He shoved us, pawed us with the back of his hand, as an irked bear might smack a cub, not to injure, just to clear a space. I can see him grabbing Mother by the hair as she cowers on a chair during a nightly quarrel. He twists her neck back until she gapes up at him, and then he lifts over her skull a glass quart bottle of milk, the milk running down his forearm, and he yells at her, "Say just one more word, one goddamn word, and I'll shut you up!" I fear she will prick him with her sharp tongue, but she is terrified into silence, and so am I, and the leaking bottle quivers in the air, and milk slithers through the red hair of my father's uplifted arm, and the entire scene is there to this moment, the head jerked back, the club raised.

When the drink made him weepy, Father would

pack a bag and kiss each of us children on the head, and announce from the front door that he was moving out. "Where to?" we demanded, fearful each time that he would leave for good, as Mr. Sampson had roared away for good in his diesel truck. "Someplace where I won't get hounded every minute," Father would answer, his jaw quivering. He stabbed a look at Mother, who might say, "Don't run into the ditch before you get there," or, "Good riddance," and then he would slink away. Mother watched him go with arms crossed over her chest, her face closed like the lid on a box of snakes. We children bawled. Where could he go? To the truck stop, that den of iniquity? To one of those dark, ratty flophouses in town? Would he wind up sleeping under a railroad bridge or on a park bench or in a cardboard box, mummied in rags, like the bums we had seen on our trips to Cleveland and Chicago? We bawled and bawled, wondering if he would ever come back.

He always did come back, a day or a week later, but each time there was a sliver less of him.

In Kafka's *The Metamorphosis*, which opens famously with Gregor Samsa waking up from uneasy dreams to find himself transformed into an insect, Gregor's family keep reassuring themselves that things will be just fine again, "When he comes back to us." Each time alcohol transformed our father, we held out the same hope, that he would really and truly come back to us, our authentic father, the tender and playful and competent man, and then all things would be fine. We had grounds for such hope. After his weepy departures and chapfallen returns, he would sometimes go weeks, even months without drinking. Those were glad times. Joy banged inside my ribs. Every day without the furtive glint of bottles, every meal without a fight, every bedtime without sobs encouraged us to believe that such bliss might go on forever.

Mother was fooled by just such a hope all during the forty-odd years she knew this Greeley Ray Sanders. Soon after she met him in a Chicago delicatessen on the eve of World War II, and fell for his butter-melting Mississippi drawl and his wavy red hair, she learned that he drank heavily. But then so did a lot of men. She would soon coax or scold him into breaking the nasty habit. She would point out to him how ugly and foolish it was, this bleary drinking, and then he would quit. He refused to quit during their engagement, however, still refused during the first years of marriage, refused until my sister came along. The shock of fatherhood sobered him, and he remained sober through my birth at the end of the war and right on through until we moved in 1951 to the Ohio arsenal, that paradise of bombs. Like all places that make a business of death, the arsenal had more than its share of alcoholics and drug addicts and other varieties of escape artists. There I turned six and started school and woke into a child's flickering awareness, just in time to see my father begin sneaking swigs in the garage.

He sobered up again for most of a year at the height of the Korean War, to celebrate the birth of my brother. But aside from that dry spell, his only breaks from drinking before I graduated from high school were just long enough to raise and then dash our hopes. Then during the fall of my senior year—the time of the Cuban missile crisis, when it seemed that the nightly explosions at the munitions dump and the nightly rages in our household might spread to engulf the globe—Father collapsed. His liver, kidneys, and heart all conked out. The doctors saved him, but only by a hair. He stayed in the hospital for weeks, going through a withdrawal so terrible that Mother would not let us visit him. If he wanted to kill himself, the doctors solemnly warned him, all he had to do was hit the bottle again. One binge would finish him.

Father must have believed them, for he stayed dry the next fifteen years. It was an answer to prayer, Mother said, it was a miracle. I believe it was a reflex of fear, which he sustained over the years through courage and pride. He knew a man could die from drink, for his brother Roscoe had. We children never laid eyes on doomed Uncle Roscoe, but in the stories Mother told us he became a fairy-tale figure, like a boy who took the wrong turning in the woods and was gobbled up by the wolf.

The fifteen-year dry spell came to an end with Father's retirement in the spring of 1978. Like many men, he gave up his identity along with his job. One day he was a boss at the factory, with a brass plate on his door and a reputation to uphold; the next day he was a nobody at home. He and Mother were leaving Ontario, the last of the many places to which his job had carried them, and they were moving to a new house in Mississippi, his childhood stomping grounds. As a boy in Mississippi, Father sold Coca-Cola during dances while the moonshiners peddled their brew in the parking lot; as a young blade, he fought in bars and in the ring, seeking a state Golden Gloves championship; he gambled at poker, hunted pheasants, raced motorcycles and cars, played semiprofessional baseball, and, along with all his buddies—in the Black Cat Saloon, behind the cotton gin, in the woods—he drank. It was a perilous youth to dream of recovering.

After his final day of work, Mother drove on ahead with a car full of begonias and violets, while Father stayed behind to oversee the packing. When the van was loaded, the sweaty movers broke open a six-pack and offered him a beer.

"Let's drink to retirement!" they crowed. "Let's drink to freedom! to fishing! hunting! loafing! Let's drink to a guy who's going home!"

At least I imagine some such words, for that is all I can do, imagine, and I see Father's hand trembling in midair as he thinks about the fifteen sober years and about the doctors' warning, and he tells himself *Goddamnit, I am a free man,* and *Why can't a free man drink one beer after a lifetime of hard work?* and I see his arm reaching, his fingers closing, the can tilting to his lips. I even supply a label for the beer, a swaggering brand that promises on television to deliver the essence of life. I watch the amber liquid pour down his throat, the alcohol steal into his blood, the key turn in his brain.

SOON AFTER MY PARENTS moved back to Father's treacherous stomping ground, my wife and I visited them in Mississippi with our five-year-old daughter. Mother had been too distraught to warn me about the return of the demons. So when I climbed out of the car that bright July morning and saw my father napping in the hammock, I felt uneasy, for in all his sober years I had never known him to sleep in daylight. Then he lurched up-right, blinked his bloodshot eyes, and greeted us in a syrupy voice. I was hurled back helpless into childhood.

"What's the matter with Papaw?" our daughter asked.

"Nothing," I said. "Nothing!"

Like a child again, I pretended not to see him in his stupor, and behind my phony smile I grieved. On that visit and on the few that remained before his death, once again I found bottles in the workbench, bottles in the woods. Again his hands shook too much for him to run a saw, to make his precious miniature furniture, to drive straight down back roads. Again he wound up in the ditch, in the hospital, in jail, in treatment centers. Again he shouted and wept. Again he lied. "I never touched a drop," he swore. "Your mother's making it up."

I no longer fancied I could reason with the men whose names I found on the bottles—Jim Beam, Jack Daniels—nor did I hope to save my father by burning down a store. I was able now to press the cold statistics about alcoholism against the ache of memory: ten mil-lion victims, fifteen million, twenty. And yet, in spite of my age, I reacted in the same blind way as I had in childhood, ignoring biology, forgetting numbers, vainly seeking to erase through my efforts whatever drove him to drink. I worked on their place twelve and sixteen hours a day, in the swelter of Mississippi summers, dig-ging ditches, running electrical wires, planting trees, mowing grass, building sheds, as though what nagged at him was some list of chores, as though by taking his worries on my shoulders I could redeem him. I was flung back into boyhood, acting as though my father would not drink himself to death if only I were perfect.

I failed of perfection; he succeeded in dying. To the end, he considered himself not sick but sinful. "Do you want to kill yourself?" I asked him. "Why not?" he answered. "Why the hell not? What's there to save?" To the end, he would not speak about his feelings, would not or could not give a name to the beast that was devouring him.

In silence, he went rushing off the cliff. Unlike the biblical swine, however, he left behind a few of the demons to haunt his children. Life with him and the loss of him twisted us into shapes that will be familiar to other sons and daughters of alcoholics. My brother became a rebel, my sister retreated into shyness, I played the stalwart and dutiful son who would hold the family together. If my father was unstable, I would be a rock. If he squandered money on drink, I would pinch every penny. If he wept when drunk—and only when drunk— I would not let myself weep at all. If he roared at the Little League umpire for calling my pitches balls, I would throw nothing but strikes. Watching him flounder and rage, I came to dread the loss of control. I would go through life without making anyone mad. I vowed never to put in my mouth or veins any chemical that would banish my everyday self. I would never make a scene, never lash out at the ones I loved, never hurt a soul. Through hard work, relentless work, I would achieve something dazzling—in the classroom, on the basketball floor, in the science lab, in the pages of books—and my achievement would distract the world's eyes from his humiliation. I would become a worthy sacrifice, and the smoke of my burning would please God.

It is far easier to recognize these twists in my character than to undo them. Work has become an addiction for me, as drink was an addiction for my father. Knowing this, my daughter gave me a placard for the wall: WORK-AHOLIC. The labor is endless and futile, for I can no more redeem myself through work than I could redeem my father. I still panic in the face of other people's anger, because his drunken temper was so terrible. I shrink from causing sadness or disappointment even to strangers, as though I were still concealing the family shame. I still notice every twitch of emotion in the faces around me, having learned as a child to read the weather in faces, and I blame myself for their least pang of unhappiness or anger. In certain moods I blame myself for everything. Guilt burns like acid in my veins.

I AM MOVED TO WRITE these pages now because my own son, at the age of ten, is taking on himself the griefs of the world, and in particular the griefs of his father. He tells me that when I am gripped by sadness he feels responsible; he feels there must be something he can do to spring me from depression, to fix my life. And that crushing sense of responsibility is exactly what I felt at the age of ten in the face of my father's drinking. My son wonders if I, too, am possessed. I write, therefore, to drag into the light what eats at me—the fear, the guilt, the shame—so that my own children may be spared.

I still shy away from nightclubs, from bars, from parties where the solvent is alcohol. My friends puzzle over this, but it is no more peculiar than for a man to shy away from the lions' den after seeing his father torn apart. I took my own first drink at the age of twenty-one, half a glass of burgundy. I knew the odds of my becoming an alcoholic were four times higher than for the sons of nonalcoholic fathers. So I sipped warily.

I still do—once a week, perhaps, a glass of wine, a can of beer, nothing stronger, nothing more. I listen for the turning of a key in my brain.

REASONS

OF THE

BODY

MY SON HAS NEVER MET A SPORT HE DID NOT LIKE. I
have met a few that left an ugly tingle—boxing and ro-
deo and pistol shooting, among others—but, then, I
have been meeting them for forty-four years, Jesse only
for twelve. Our ages are relevant to the discussion, because, on the hill of the sporting life, Jesse is midway up
the slope and climbing rapidly, while I am over the crest
and digging in my heels as I slip down.

"You still get around pretty well for an old guy," he
told me last night after we had played catch in the park.

The catch we play has changed subtly in recent
months, a change that dramatizes a shift in the forces
binding father and son. Early on, when I was a decade
younger and Jesse a toddler, I was the agile one, leaping

to snare his wild throws. The ball we tossed in those days was rubbery and light, a bubble of air as big around as a soup bowl, easy for small hands to grab. By the time he started school, we were using a tennis ball, then we grad-uated to a softball, then to gloves and a baseball. His repertoire of catches and throws increased along with his vocabulary.

Over the years, as Jesse put on inches and pounds and grace, I still had to be careful how far and hard I threw, to avoid bruising his ribs or his pride. But this spring, when we began limbering up our arms, his throws came whistling at me with a zing that hurt my hand, and he caught effortlessly anything I could hurl back at him. It was as though the food he wolfed down all winter had turned into spring steel. I no longer needed to hold back. Now Jesse is the one, when he is feeling charita-ble, who pulls his pitches.

Yesterday in the park, he was feeling frisky rather than charitable. We looped the ball lazily back and forth awhile. Then he started backing away, backing away, until my shoulder twinged from the length of throws. Unsatisfied, he yelled, "Make me run for it!" So I flung the ball high and deep, low and wide, driving him over the grass, yet he loped easily wherever it flew, gathered it in, then whipped it back to me with stinging speed.

"Come on," he yelled, "put it where I can't reach it." I tried, ignoring the ache in my arm, and still he ran under the ball. He might have been gliding on a cushion of air, he moved so lightly. I was feeling heavy, and felt heavier by the minute as his return throws, grown sud-denly and unaccountably wild, forced me to hustle back and forth, jump and dive.

"Hey," I yelled, waving my glove at him, "look where I'm standing!"

"Standing is right," he yelled back. "Let's see those legs move!" His next throw sailed over my head, and the ones after that sailed farther still, now left now right, out of my range, until I gave up even trying for them, and the ball thudded accusingly to the ground. By the time we quit, I was sucking air, my knees were stiffening, and my arm was ablaze with pain. Jesse trotted up, his T-shirt dry, his breathing casual. This was the moment he chose to clap me on the back and say, "You still get around pretty well for an old guy."

It was a line I might have delivered, as a cocky teenager, to my own father. In his sober hours and years, which are the hours and years I measure him by, he would have laughed and then challenged me to a round of golf or a bout of arm wrestling, contests he could still easily have won.

Whatever else these games may be, they are always contests. For many a boy, some playing field, some court or gym is the first arena in which he can outstrip his old man. For me, the arena was a concrete driveway, where I played basketball against my father, shooting at a rusty hoop that was mounted over the garage. He had taught me how to dribble, how to time my jump, how to follow through on my shots. To begin with, I could barely heave the ball to the basket, and he would applaud if I so much as banged the rim. I banged away, year by year, my bones lengthening, muscles thickening. I shuffled over the concrete to the jazz of bird song and the opera of thunderstorms. I practiced fervently, as though my life depended on putting the ball through the hoop, practiced when the driveway was dusted with pollen and when it was drifted with snow. From first light to twilight, while the chimney swifts spiraled out to feed on mosquitoes and the mosquitoes fed on me, I kept shooting, hour after hour. Many of those hours, Father was tinkering in the garage, which reverberated with the slap of my feet and the slam of the ball. There came a day when I realized that I could outleap him, outhustle and outshoot him. I began to notice his terrible breathing, terrible because I had not realized he could run short of air. I had not realized he could run short of anything. When he bent over and grabbed his knees, huffing, "You're too much for me," I felt at once triumphant and dismayed.

I still have to hold back when playing basketball with Jesse. But the day will come, and soon, when he grows taller and stronger, and he will be the one to show mercy. The only dessert I will be able to eat, if I am to avoid growing fat, will be humble pie. Even now my shots appear old-fashioned to him, as my father's arching two-handed heaves seemed antique to me. "Show me some of those Neanderthal moves," Jesse cries as we shoot around at a basket in the park. "Show me how they did it in the Stone Age!" I do show him, clowning and hot-dogging, wishing by turns to amuse and impress him. As I fake and spin, I am simultaneously father and son, playing games forward and backward in time.

THE GAME OF CATCH, like other sports where body faces body, is a dialogue carried on with muscle and bone. One body speaks by throwing a ball or a punch, by lunging with a foil, smashing a backhand, kicking a shot toward the corner of the net; the other replies by swinging, leaping, dodging, tackling, parrying, balancing. As in lovemaking, this exchange may be a struggle for power or a sharing of pleasure. The call and response may be in the spirit of antiphonal singing, a making of music that neither person could have achieved alone, or it may be in the spirit of insults bellowed across a table.

When a father and son play sports, especially a game the son has learned from the father, every motive from bitter rivalry to mutual delight may enter in. At first eagerly, and then grudgingly, and at last unconsciously, the son watches how his father grips the ball, handles the glove, swings the bat. In just the same way, the son has watched how the father swings a hammer, how the father walks, jokes, digs, starts a car, gentles a horse, pays a bill, shakes hands, shaves. There is a season in one's growing up, beginning at about the age Jesse is now, when a son comes to feel his old man's example as a smothering weight. You must shrug free of it, or die. And so, if your father carries himself soldier straight, you begin to slouch; if he strides along with a swagger, you slink; if he talks in joshing Mississippi accents to anybody with ears, you shun strangers and swallow your drawl. With luck and time, you may come to accept that you bear in your own voice overtones of your father's. You may come to rejoice that your own least motion—kissing a baby or opening a jar—is informed by memories of how your father would have done it. Between the early delight and the late reconciliation, however, you must pass through that season of rivalry, the son striving

to undo or outdo his father's example, the father chewing on the bitter rind of rejection.

WHY DO I SPEAK only of boys and men? Because, while
there are females aplenty who relish any sport you can
name, I have never shared a roof with one. In her sev-
enties, my mother still dances and swims, even leads
classes in aerobics, but she's never had much use for
games played with balls, and neither has my wife or
daughter. When Ruth, my wife, was a child, a bout of
rheumatic fever confined her to bed and then to a wheel-
chair for several years. Until she was old enough for university, a heart rendered tricky by the illness kept her
from doing anything that would raise her pulse, and by
then she had invested her energies elsewhere, in music
and science. To this day, Ruth sees no point in moving
faster than a walk, or in defying gravity with exuberant
leaps, or in puzzling over the trajectory of a ball.

And what of our daughter, sprightly Eva, firstborn?
Surely I could have brought her up to become a partner
for catch? Let me assure you that I tried. I put a sponge
ball in her crib, as Father had put a baseball in mine. (I
was going to follow tradition exactly and teethe her on
a baseball, but Ruth, sensible of a baby's delicacy, said
nothing doing.) From the moment the nurse handed Eva
to me in the hospital, a quivering bundle, ours to keep,
I coached my spunky girl, I coaxed and exhorted her,
but she would not be persuaded that throwing or shooting or kicking a ball was a sensible way to spend an hour
or an afternoon. After seventeen years of all the en-

couragement that love can buy, the one sport she will deign to play with me is volleyball, in which she hurtles over the grass, leaping and cavorting, as only a dancer could.

As a dancer and gymnast, Eva has always been on good terms with her body, and yet, along with her mother and my mother, she rolls her eyes when Jesse and I begin rummaging in the battered box on the porch for a baseball, basketball, or soccer ball. "So Dad," she calls, "it's off to recover past glories, is it? You show 'em, tiger. But don't break any bones."

Eva's amusement has made the opinion of the women in my life unanimous. Their baffled indulgence, bordering at times on mockery, has given to sports a tang of the mildly illicit.

Like many other women (not all, not all), those in my family take even less interest in talking about sports than in playing them. They pride themselves on being above such idle gab. They shake their heads when my son and I check the scores in the newspaper. They are astounded that we can spend longer rehashing a game than we spent in playing it. When Jesse and I compare aches after a session on field or court, the women observe mildly that it sounds as though we had been mugged. Surely we would not inflict such damage on ourselves? Perhaps we have gotten banged up from wrestling bears? We kid along and say, "Yes, we ran into the Chicago Bears," and my daughter or mother or wife will reply, "You mean the hockey team?"

In many households and offices, gossip about games and athletes breaks down along gender lines, the men indulging in it and the women scoffing. Those on each side of the line may exaggerate their feelings, the men pumping up their enthusiasm, the women their indifference, until sport becomes a male mystery. No locker room, no sweat lodge is needed to shut women out; mere talk will do it. Men are capable of muttering about wins and losses, batting averages and slam dunks, until the flowers on the wallpaper begin to wilt and every woman in the vicinity begins to yearn for a supply of gags. A woman friend of mine, an executive in a computing firm, has been driven in self-defense to scan the headlines of the sports pages before going to work, so that she can toss out references to the day's contests and stars, like chunks of meat, to feed the appetites of her male colleagues. After gnawing on this bait, the men may consent to speak with her of things more in keeping with her taste, such as books, birds, and the human condition.

MY DAUGHTER HAS NEVER allowed me to buy her a single item of sports paraphernalia. My son, on the other hand, has never said no to such an offer. Day and night, visions of athletic gear dance in his head. With religious zeal, he pores over magazine ads for sneakers, examining the stripes and insignia as if they were hieroglyphs of ultimate truth. Between us, Jesse and I are responsible for the hoard of equipment on our back porch, which contains at present the following items: one bicycle helmet and two bicycles; a volleyball set, badminton set, and a bag of golf clubs; three racquets for tennis, two for squash, one for paddleball; roller skates and ice skates, together with a pair of hockey sticks; goalie gloves, batting gloves, three baseball gloves and one catcher's mitt; numerous yo-yos; ten pairs of cleated or waffle-soled shoes; a drying rack festooned with shorts and socks and shirts and sweatsuits; and a cardboard box heaped with (I counted) forty-nine balls, including ones for all the sports implicated above, as well as for Ping-Pong, lacrosse, juggling, and jacks.

Excavated by some future archaeologist, this porch full of gear would tell as much about how we passed our lives as would the shells and seeds and bones of a kitchen midden. An excavation of the word *sport* also yields evidence of breaks, bruises, and ambiguities. A sport is a game, an orderly zone marked off from the prevailing disorder, but it can also be a mutation, a violation of rules. To be good at sports is to be a winner, and yet a good sport is one who loses amiably, a bad sport one who kicks and screams at every setback. A flashy dresser might be called a sport, and so might a gambler, an idler, an easygoing companion, one who dines high on the hog of pleasure. But the same label may be attached to one who is the butt of jokes, a laughingstock, a goat. As a verb, to sport can mean to wear jewelry or clothes in a showy manner, to poke fun, to trifle, to roll promiscuously in the hay. It is a word spiced with unsavory meanings, rather tacky and cheap, with hints of brothels, speakeasies, and malodorous dives. And yet it bears also the wholesome flavor of fairness, vigor, and ease.

THE LORE OF SPORTS may be all that some fathers have to pass down to their sons in place of lore about hunting animals, planting seeds, killing enemies, or placating the

gods. Instead of telling him how to shoot a buffalo, the
father whispers in the son's ear how to shoot a lay-up.
Instead of consulting the stars or the entrails of birds,
father and son consult the smudged print of newspapers
to see how their chosen spirits are faring. They fiddle
with the dials of radios, hoping to catch the oracular
murmur of a distant game. The father recounts heroic
deeds, not from the field of battle, but from the field of
play. The seasons about which he speaks lead not to har-
vests but to championships. No longer intimate with the
wilderness, no longer familiar even with the tamed land
of farms, we create artificial landscapes bounded by lines
of paint or lime. Within those boundaries, as within the
frame of a chessboard or painting, life achieves a mem-
orable, seductive clarity. The lore of sports is a step down
from that of nature, perhaps even a tragic step, but it is
lore nonetheless, with its own demigods and demons,
magic and myths.

The sporting legends I carry from my father are private rather than public. I am haunted by scenes that no
journalist recorded, no camera filmed. Father is playing
a solo round of golf, for example, early one morning in
April. The fairways glisten with dew. Crows rasp and
fluster in the pines that border the course. Father lofts
a shot toward a par-3 hole, and the white ball arcs over
the pond, over the sand trap, over the shaggy apron of
grass onto the green, where it bounces, settles down,
then rolls toward the flag, rolls unerringly, inevitably,
until it falls with a scarcely audible click into the hole.
The only eyes within sight besides his own are the
crows'. For once, the ball has obeyed him perfectly, har-
monizing wind and gravity and the revolution of the

33

spheres, one shot has gone where all are meant to go, and there is nobody else to watch. He stands on the tee, gazing at the distant hole, knowing what he has done and that he will never do it again. The privacy of this moment appeals to me more than all the clamor and fame of a shot heard round the world.

Here is another story I live by: the man who will become my father is twenty-two, a catcher for a bush-league baseball team in Tennessee. He will never make it to the majors, but on weekends he earns a few dollars for squatting behind the plate and nailing runners foolish enough to try stealing second base. From all those bus rides, all those red-dirt diamonds, the event he will describe for his son with deepest emotion is an exhibition game. Father's team of whites, most of them fresh from two-mule farms, is playing a touring black team, a rare event for that day and place. To make it even rarer, and the sides fairer, the coaches agree to mix the teams. And so my father, son of a Mississippi cotton farmer, bruised with racial notions that will take a lifetime to heal, crouches behind the plate and for nine innings catches fastballs and curves, change-ups and screwballs from a whirling, muttering wizard of the Negro Baseball League, one Leroy Robert Paige, known to the world as Satchel. Afterward, Satchel Paige tells the farm boy, "You catch a good game," and the farm boy answers, "You've got the stuff, mister." And for the rest of my father's life, this man's pitching serves as a measure of mastery.

And here is a third myth I carry: One evening when the boy who will become my father is eighteen, he walks into the Black Cat Saloon in Tupelo, Mississippi. He is looking for a fight. Weary of plowing, sick of red dirt, baffled by his own turbulent energy, he often picks fights. This evening the man he picks on is a stranger who occupies a nearby stool at the bar, a husky man in his thirties, wearing a snap-brim hat, dark suit with wide lapels, narrow tie, and an infuriatingly white shirt. The stranger is slow to anger. The red-headed Sanders boy keeps at him, keeps at him, mocking the Yankee accent, the hat worn indoors, the monkey suit, the starched shirt, until at last the man stands up and backs away from the bar, fists raised. The Sanders boy lands three punches, he remembers that much, but the next thing he remembers is waking up on the sidewalk, the stranger bending over him to ask if he is all right, and to ask, besides, if he would like a boxing scholarship to Mississippi State. The man is headed there to become the new coach. The boy who will become my father goes to Mississippi State for two years, loses some bouts and wins more, then quits to pursue a Golden Gloves title. When he fails at that, he keeps on fighting in bars and streets, until at last he quits boxing, his nose broken so many times there is no bone left in it, only a bulb of flesh which a boy sitting in his lap will later squeeze and mash like dough. From all those bouts, the one he will describe to his son with the greatest passion is that brawl from the Black Cat Saloon, when the stranger in the white shirt, a good judge of fighters, found him worthy.

FATHER TRIED, with scant success, to make a boxer of me. Not for a career in the ring, he explained, but for defense against the roughs and rowdies who would cross my path in life. If I ran into a mean customer, I told him, I could always get off the path. No, Father said, a man never backs away. A man stands his ground and fights. This advice ran against my grain, which inclined toward quickness of wits rather than fists, yet for years I strove to become the tough guy he envisioned. Without looking for fights, I stumbled into them at every turn, in schoolyard and backyard and in the shadows of barns. Even at my most belligerent, I still tried cajolery and oratory first. Only when that failed did I dig in my heels and start swinging. I gave bruises and received them, gave and received bloody noses, leading with my left, as Father had taught me, protecting my head with fore-arms, keeping my thumbs outside my balled fists to avoid breaking them when I landed a punch.

Some bullies saw my feistiness as a red flag. One boy who kept hounding me was Olaf Magnuson, a neighbor whose surname I would later translate with my primitive Latin as Son of Big. The name was appropriate, for Olaf was two years older and a foot taller and forty pounds heavier than I was. He pestered me, cursed me, irked and insulted me. When I stood my ground, he pounded me into it. One evening in my twelfth summer, after I had staggered home several times from these frays blood-ied and bowed, Father decided it was time for serious boxing lessons. We would train for two months, he told me, then challenge Olaf Magnuson to a fight, complete with gloves and ropes and bell. This did not sound like a healthy idea to me; but Father insisted. "Do you want to keep getting pushed around," he demanded, "or are you going to lick the tar out of him?"

Every day for two months I ran, skipped rope, did

chin-ups and push-ups. Father hung his old punching bag from a rafter in the basement, and I flailed at it until my arms filled with sand. He wrapped an old mattress around a tree and told me to imagine Olaf Magnuson's belly as I pounded the cotton ticking. I sparred with my grizzly old man, who showed me how to jab and hook, duck and weave, how to keep my balance and work out of corners. Even though his feet had slowed, his hands were still so quick that I sometimes dropped my own gloves to watch him, dazzled. "Keep up those dukes," he warned. "Never lower your guard." For two months I trained as though I had a boxer's heart.

Father issued our challenge by way of Olaf Magnuson's father, a strapping man with a voice like a roar in a barrel. Hell yes, my boy'll fight, the elder Magnuson boomed.

On the morning appointed for our bout, Father strung rope from tree to tree in the yard, fashioning a ring that was shaped like a lozenge. My mother, who had been kept in the dark about the grudge match until that morning, raised sand for a while; failing to make us see what fools we were, disgusted with the ways of men, she drove off to buy groceries. My sister carried word through the neighborhood, and within minutes a gaggle of kids and a scattering of bemused adults pressed against the ropes.

"You're going to make that lunkhead bawl in front of the whole world," Father told me in the kitchen while lacing my gloves. "You're going to make him call for his mama. Before you're done with him, he's going to swallow so many teeth that he'll never mess with you again."

So long as Father was talking, I believed him. I was

a mean hombre. I was bad news, one fist of iron and the other one steel. When he finished his pep talk, however, and we stepped out into the sunshine, and I saw the crowd buzzing against the ropes, and I spied enormous Olaf slouching from his own kitchen door, my confidence hissed away like water on a hot griddle. In the seconds it took me to reach the ring, I ceased to feel like the bringer of bad news and began to feel like the imminent victim. I danced in my corner, eyeing Olaf. His torso, hulking above jeans and clodhopper boots, made my own scrawny frame look like a preliminary sketch for a body. I glanced down at my ropy arms, at my twiggy legs exposed below red gym shorts, at my hightopped basketball shoes, at the grass.

"He'll be slow," Father growled in my ear, "slow and clumsy. Keep moving. Bob and weave. Give him that left jab, watch for an opening, and then *bam*, unload with the right."

Not trusting my voice, I nodded, and kept shuffling my sneakers to hide the shivers.

Father put his palms to my cheeks and drew my face close to his and looked hard at me. Above that smushed, boneless nose, his brown eyes were as dark and shiny as those of a deer. "You okay, big guy?" he asked. "You ready for this?" I nodded again. "Then go get him," he said, turning me around and giving me a light shove toward the center of the ring.

I met Olaf there for instructions from the referee, a welder who lived down the road from us, a wiry man with scorched forearms who had just fixed our trailer hitch. I lifted my eyes reluctantly from Olaf's boots, along the trunks of his jean-clad legs, over the expanse of brawny chest and palooka jaw to his ice blue eyes. They seemed less angry than amused.

A cowbell clattered. Olaf and I touched gloves, backed apart and lifted our mitts. The crowd sizzled against the ropes. Blood banged in my ears, yet I could hear Father yelling. I hear him still. And in memory I follow his advice. I bob, I weave, I guard my face with curled gloves, I feint and jab within the roped diamond, I begin to believe in myself, I circle my lummoxy rival and pepper him with punches, I feel a grin rising to my lips, and then Olaf tires of the game and rears back and knocks me flat. He also knocks me out. He also breaks my nose, which will remain crooked forever after.

That ended my boxing career. Olaf quit bullying me, perhaps because my blackout had given him a scare, perhaps because he had proved whatever he needed to prove. What I had shown my father was less clear. He may have seen weakness, may have seen a doomed and reckless bravery, may have seen a clown's pratfall. In any case, he never again urged me to clear the path with my fists.

And I have not offered boxing lessons to my son. Instead, I offered him the story of my defeat. When Jesse would still fit in my lap, I cuddled him there and told of my fight with Olaf, and he ran his delicate finger against the crook in my nose, as I had fingered the boneless pulp of Father's nose. I told Jesse about learning to play catch, the ball passing back and forth like a thread between my father and me, stitching us together. I told him about the time one of my pitches sailed over Father's head and shattered the windshield of our 1956 Ford, a car just three days old, and Father only shook his head and said, "Shoot, boy, you get that fastball down, and the batters won't see a thing but smoke." And I told Jesse about sitting on a feather tick in a Mississippi farmhouse, wedged between my father and grandfather, shaking with their excitement while before us on a tiny black-and-white television two boxers slammed and hugged each other. Cradling my boy, I felt how difficult it is for men to embrace without the liquor of violence, the tonic of pain.

WHY DO WE PLAY these games so avidly? All sports, viewed dispassionately, are dumb. The rules are arbitrary, the behaviors absurd. For boxing and running, perhaps, you could figure out evolutionary advantages. But what earthly use is it to become expert at swatting a ball with a length of wood or at lugging an inflated pigskin through a mob? Freudians might say that in playing with balls we men are simply toying with the prize portion of our anatomies. Darwinians might claim that we are competing for the attention of females, like so many preening peacocks or head-butting rams. Physicians might attribute the sporting frenzy to testosterone; economists might point to our dreams of professional paychecks; feminists might appeal to our machismo; philosophers, to our fear of death.

No doubt all of those explanations, like buckets put out in the rain, catch some of the truth. But none of them catches all of the truth. None of them explains, for example, what moves a boy to bang a rubber ball against a wall for hours, for entire summers, as my father did in his youth, as I did in mine, as Jesse still does. That boy, throwing and catching in the lee of garage or barn, dwells for a time wholly in his body, and that is reward enough. He aims the ball at a knothole, at a crack, then leaps to snag the rebound, mastering a skill, working himself into a trance. How different is his rapture from the dancing and drumming of a young brave? How different is his solitude from that of any boy seeking visions?

The less use we have for our bodies, the more we need reminding that the body possesses its own way of knowing. To steal a line from Pascal: The body has its reasons that reason knows nothing of. Although we struggle lifelong to dwell in the flesh without rancor, without division between act and desire, we succeed only for moments at a time. We treasure whatever brings us those moments, whether it be playing cello or playing pool, making love or making baskets, kneading bread or nursing a baby or kicking a ball. Whoever teaches us an art or skill, whoever shows us a path to momentary wholeness, deserves our love.

I am conscious of my father's example whenever I teach a game to my son. Demonstrating a move in basketball, I amplify my gestures, like a ham actor playing to the balcony. My pleasure in the part is increased by the knowledge that others, and especially Father, have played it before me. What I know about hitting a curve or shooting a hook shot or throwing a left jab, I know less by words than by feel. When I take Jesse's hand and curl his fingers over the baseball's red stitches, explaining how to make it deviously spin, I feel my father's hands slip over mine like gloves. Move like so, like so. I feel the same ghostly guidance when I hammer nails

or fix a faucet or pluck a banjo. Working on the house
or garden or car, I find myself wearing more than my
father's hands, find myself clad entirely in his skin.

One blistering afternoon when I was a year younger
than Jesse is now, a fly ball arched toward me in center
field. I ran under it, lifted my face and glove, and lost
the ball in the sun. The ball found me, however, crashing into my eye. In the split second before blacking out
I saw nothing but light. We need not go hunting pain,
for pain will find us. It hurts me more to see Jesse ache
than to break one of my own bones. I cry out as the
ground ball bangs into his throat. I wince as he comes
down crookedly with a rebound and turns his ankle. I
wish to spare him injury as I wish to spare him defeat,
but I could not do so even if I had never lobbed him
that first fat pitch.

As Jesse nears thirteen, his estimate of my knowledge and my power declines rapidly. He sees me slipping
down the far slope. If I were a potter, say, or a carpenter,
my skills would outreach his for decades to come. But
where speed and stamina are the essence, a father in his
forties will be overtaken by a son in his teens. Training
for soccer, Jesse carries a stopwatch as he jogs around
the park. I am not training for anything, only knocking
rust from my joints and beguiling my heart, but I run
along with him, puffing to keep up. I know that his times
will keep going down, while I will never run faster than
I do now. This is as it should be, for his turn has come.
Slow as I am, and doomed to be slower, I relish his company.

In the game of catch, this dialogue of throw and grab
we have been carrying on since he was old enough to

crawl, Jesse has finally begun to put questions that I cannot answer. I know the answers; I can see how my back should twist, my legs should pump; but legs and back will no longer match my vision. This faltering is the condition of our lives, of course, a condition that will grow more acute with each passing year. I mean to live the present year before rushing off to any future ones. I mean to keep playing games with my son, so long as flesh will permit, as my father played games with me well past his own physical prime. Now that sports have begun to give me lessons in mortality, I realize they have also been giving me, all the while, lessons in immortality. These games, these contests, these grunting conversations of body to body, father to son, are not substitutes for some other way of being alive. They are the sweet and sweaty thing itself.

LOOKING
AT WOMEN

ON THAT SIZZLING JULY AFTERNOON, THE GIRL WHO
crossed at the stoplight in front of our car looked, as my
mother would say, as though she had been poured into
her pink shorts. The girl's matching pink halter bared
her stomach and clung to her nubbin breasts, leaving
little to the imagination, as my mother would also say.
Until that moment, it had never made any difference to
me how much or little a girl's clothing revealed, for my
imagination had been entirely devoted to other mysteries. I was eleven. The girl was about fourteen, the age
of my buddy Norman who lounged in the back seat with
me. Staring after her, Norman elbowed me in the ribs
and murmured, "Check out that chassis."

His mother glared around from the driver's seat. "Hush your mouth."

"I was talking about that sweet Chevy," said Norman, pointing out a souped-up jalopy at the curb.

"I know what you were talking about," his mother snapped.

No doubt she did know, since mothers could read minds, but at first I myself did not have a clue. Chassis? I knew what it meant for a car, an airplane, a radio, or even a cannon to have a chassis. But could a girl have one as well? I glanced after the retreating figure, and suddenly noticed with a sympathetic twitching in my belly the way her long raven ponytail swayed in rhythm to her walk and the way her fanny jostled in those pink shorts. In July's dazzle of sun, her swinging legs and arms flashed at me a code I could almost read.

As the light turned green and our car pulled away, Norman's mother cast one more scowl at her son in the rearview mirror, saying, "Just think how it makes her feel to have you two boys gawking at her."

How? I wondered.

"Makes her feel like hot stuff," said Norman, owner of a bold mouth.

"If you don't get your mind out of the gutter, you're going to wind up in the state reformatory," said his mother.

Norman gave a snort. I sank into the seat, and tried to figure out what power had sprung from that sashaying girl to zap me in the belly.

Only after much puzzling did it dawn on me that I must finally have drifted into the force field of sex, as a space traveler who has lived all his years in free-fall might rocket for the first time within gravitational reach of a star. Even as a bashful eleven-year-old I knew the word *sex,* of course, and I could paste that name across my image of the tantalizing girl. But a label for a mystery no more explains a mystery than the word *gravity* explains gravity. As I grew a beard and my taste shifted from girls to women, I acquired a more cagey language for speaking of desire. I picked up disarming theories. First by hearsay and then by experiment, I learned the delicious details of making babies. I came to appreciate the urgency for propagation that litters the road with maple seeds and drives salmon up waterfalls and yokes the newest crop of boys to the newest crop of girls. Books in their killjoy wisdom taught me that all the valentines and violins, the waltzes and glances, the long fever and ache of romance were merely embellishments on biology's instructions that we multiply our kind. And yet, the fraction of desire that actually leads to procreation is so vanishingly small as to seem irrelevant. In his lifetime a man sways to a million longings, only a few of which, or perhaps none at all, ever lead to the fathering of children.

Now, thirty years away from that July afternoon, firmly married, twice a father, I am still humming from the power unleashed by the girl in pink shorts, still wondering how it made her feel to have two boys gawk at her, still puzzling over how to dwell in the force field of desire.

How should a man look at women? It is a peculiarly and perhaps neurotically human question. Billy goats do not fret over how they should look at nanny goats. They look or don't look, as seasons and hormones dictate, and feel what they feel without benefit of theory. There is more billy goat in most men than we care to admit. None of us, however, is pure goat. To live utterly as an animal would make the business of sex far tidier but also drearier. If we tried, like Rousseau, to peel off the layers of civilization and imagine our way back to some pristine man and woman who have not yet been corrupted by hand-me-down notions of sexuality, my hunch is that we would find, in our speculative state of nature, that men regarded women with appalling simplicity. In any case, unlike goats, we dwell in history. What attracts our eyes and rouses our blood is only partly instinctual. Other forces contend in us as well, the voices of books and religions, the images of art and film and advertising, the entire chorus of culture. Norman's telling me to relish the sight of females and his mother's telling me to keep my eyes to myself are only two of the many voices quarreling in my head.

If there were a rule book for sex, it would be longer than the one for baseball (that byzantine sport), more intricate and obscure than tax instructions from the Internal Revenue Service. What I present here are a few images and reflections that cling, for me, to this one item in such a compendium of rules: How should a man look at women?

WELL BEFORE I WAS TO SEE any women naked in the flesh, I saw a bevy of them naked in photographs, hung in a gallery around the bed of my freshman roommate at college. A *Playboy* subscriber, he would pluck the centerfold from its staples each month and tape another airbrushed lovely to the wall. The gallery was in place when I moved in, and for an instant before I realized what I was looking at, all that expanse of skin reminded me of a meat locker back in Newton Falls, Ohio. I never quite shook that first impression, even after I had inspected the pinups at my leisure on subsequent days. Every curve of buttock and breast was news to me, an innocent kid from the Puritan back roads. Today you would be hard pressed to find a college freshman as ignorant as I was of female anatomy, if only because teenagers now routinely watch movies at home that would have been shown, during my teen years, exclusively on the fly-speckled screens of honky-tonk cinemas or in the basement of the Kinsey Institute. I studied those alien shapes on the wall with a curiosity that was not wholly sexual, a curiosity tinged with the wonder that astronomers must have felt when they pored over the early photographs of the far side of the moon.

The paper women seemed to gaze back at me, enticing or mocking, yet even in my adolescent dither I was troubled by the phony stare, for I knew this was no true exchange of looks. Those mascaraed eyes were not fixed on me but on a camera. What the models felt as they posed I could only guess—perhaps the boredom of any numbskull job, perhaps the weight of dollar bills, perhaps the sweltering lights of fame, perhaps a tingle of the power that launched a thousand ships.

Whatever their motives, these women had chosen to put themselves on display. For the instant of the

photograph, they had become their bodies, as a prize-
fighter does in the moment of landing a punch, as a
weight lifter does in the moment of hoisting a barbell,
as a ballerina does in the whirl of a pirouette, as we all
do in the crisis of making love or dying. Men, ogling
such photographs, are supposed to feel that where so
much surface is revealed there can be no depths. Yet I
never doubted that behind the makeup and the plump
curves and the two dimensions of the image there was
an inwardness, a feeling self as mysterious as my own.
In fact, during moments when I should have been studying French or thermodynamics, I would glance at my
roommate's wall and invent mythical lives for those goddesses. The lives I made up were adolescent ones, to be
sure; but so was mine. Without that saving aura of inwardness, these women in the glossy photographs would
have become merely another category of objects for sale,
alongside the sports cars and stereo systems and liquors
advertised in the same pages. If not extinguished, however, their humanity was severely reduced. And if by
simplifying themselves they had lost some human essence, then by gaping at them I had shared in the theft.

What did that gaping take from me? How did it af-
fect my way of seeing other women, those who would
never dream of lying nude on a fake tiger rug before the
million-faceted eye of a camera? The bodies in the photographs were implausibly smooth and slick and inflated,
like balloon caricatures that might be floated overhead
in a parade. Free of sweat and scars and imperfections,
sensual without being fertile, tempting yet impregnable,
they were Platonic ideals of the female form, divorced

49

from time and the dither of living, excused from the perplexities of mind. No actual woman could rival their insipid perfection.

The swains who gathered to admire my roommate's gallery discussed the pinups in the same tones and in much the same language as the farmers back home in Ohio used for assessing cows. The relevant parts of male or female bodies are quickly named—and, the *Kamasutra* and Marquis de Sade notwithstanding, the number of ways in which those parts can be stimulated or conjoined is touchingly small—so these studly conversations were more tedious than chitchat about the weather. I would lie on my bunk pondering calculus or Aeschylus and unwillingly hear the same few nouns and fewer verbs issuing from one mouth after another, and I would feel smugly superior. Here I was, improving my mind, while theirs wallowed in the notorious gutter. Eventually the swains would depart, leaving me in peace, and from the intellectual heights of my bunk I would glance across at those photographs . . . and yield to the gravity of lust. Idiot flesh! How stupid that a counterfeit stare and artful curves, printed in millions of copies on glossy paper, could arouse me. But there it was, not the first proof of my body's automatism and not the last.

Nothing in men is more machinelike than the flipping of sexual switches. I have never been able to read with a straight face the claims made by D. H. Lawrence and lesser pundits that the penis is a god, a lurking dragon. It more nearly resembles a railroad crossing signal, which stirs into life at intervals to announce, "Here comes a train." Or, if the penis must be likened to an animal, let it be an ill-trained circus dog, sitting up and playing dead and heeling whenever it takes a notion, oblivious of the trainer's commands. Meanwhile, heart, lungs, blood vessels, pupils, and eyelids all assert their independence like the members of a rebellious troupe. Reason stands helpless at the center of the ring, cracking its whip.

While he was president, Jimmy Carter raised a brouhaha by confessing in a *Playboy* interview, of all shady places, that he occasionally felt lust in his heart for women. What man hasn't, aside from those who feel lust in their hearts for other men? The commentators flung their stones anyway. Naughty, naughty, they chirped. Wicked Jimmy. Perhaps Mr. Carter could derive some consolation from psychologist Allen Wheelis, who, in *The Doctor of Desire*, blames male appetite on biology: "We have been selected for desiring. Nothing could have convinced us by argument that it would be worthwhile to chase endlessly and insatiably after women, but something has transformed us from within, a plasmid has invaded our DNA, has twisted our nature so that now this is exactly what we *want* to do." Certainly, by Darwinian logic, those males who were most avid in their pursuit of females were also the most likely to pass on their genes. Consoling it may be, yet it is finally no solution to blame biology. "I am extremely sexual in my desires: I carry them everywhere and at all times," William Carlos Williams tells us on the opening page of his *Autobiography*. "I think that from that arises the drive which empowers us all. Given that drive, a man does with it what his mind directs. In the manner in which he directs that power lies his secret." I agree with the honest doctor. Whatever the contents of my DNA, however potent the influence of my ancestors, I still must direct that rebellious power. I still must live with the consequences of my looking and my longing.

ALOOF ON THEIR BLANKETS like goddesses on clouds, the pinups did not belong to my funky world. I was invisible to them, and they were immune to my gaze. Not so the women who passed me on the street, sat near me in classes, shared a table with me in the cafeteria: it was risky to stare at them. They could gaze back, and sometimes did, with looks both puzzling and exciting. It only complicated matters for me to realize that so many of these strangers had taken precautions that men should notice them. The girl in matching pink halter and shorts who set me humming in my eleventh year might only have wanted to keep cool in the sizzle of July. But these alluring college femmes had deeper designs. Perfume, eye shadow, uplift bras (about which I learned in the Sears catalog), curled hair, stockings, jewelry, lipstick, lace—what were these if not hooks tossed into male waters?

I recall being mystified in particular by spike heels. They looked painful to me, and dangerous. Danger may have been the point, since the spikes would have made good weapons—they were affectionately known, after all, as stilettos. Or danger may have been the point in another sense, because a woman teetering along on such heels is tipsy, vulnerable, broadcasting her need for support. And who better than a man to prop her up, some guy who clomps around in brogans wide enough for the cornerstones of flying buttresses? (For years after college,

I felt certain that spike heels had been forever banned, like bustles and foot binding, but lately they have come back in fashion, and once more one encounters women teetering along on knife points.)

Back in those days of my awakening to women, I was also baffled by lingerie. I do not mean underwear, the proletariat of clothing, and I do not mean foundation garments, pale and sensible. I mean what the woman who lives in the house behind ours—owner of a shop called "Bare Essentials"—refers to as "intimate apparel." Those two words announce that her merchandise is both sexy and expensive. These flimsy items cost more per ounce than truffles, more than frankincense and myrrh. They are put-ons whose only purpose is in being taken off. I have a friend who used to attend the men's-only nights at "Bare Essentials," during which he would invariably buy a slinky outfit or two, by way of proving his serious purpose, outfits that wound up in the attic because his wife would not be caught dead in them. Most of the customers at the shop are women, however, as the models are women, and the owner is a woman. What should one make of that? During my college days I knew about intimate apparel only by rumor, not being that intimate with anyone who would have tricked herself out in such finery, but I could see the spike heels and other female trappings everywhere I turned. Why, I wondered then and wonder still, do so many women decorate themselves like dolls?

On this question as on many others, Simone De Beauvoir has clarified matters for me, writing in *The Second Sex*: "The 'feminine' woman in making herself prey tries to reduce man, also, to her carnal passivity; she occupies herself in catching him in her trap, in enchaining him by means of the desires she arouses in him in submissively making herself a thing." Those women who transform themselves into dolls, in other words, do so because that is the most potent identity available to them. "It must be admitted," De Beauvoir concedes, "that the males find in woman more complicity than the oppressor usually finds in the oppressed. And in bad faith they take authorization from this to declare that she has *desired* the destiny they have imposed on her."

Complicity, oppressor, bad faith: such terms yank us into a moral realm unknown to goats. While I am saddled with enough male guilt to believe three-quarters of De Beauvoir's claim, I still doubt that men are so entirely to blame for the turning of women into sexual dolls. I believe human history is more collaborative than her argument would suggest. It seems unlikely to me that one half the species could have "imposed" a destiny on the other half, unless that other half were far more craven than the females I have known. Some women have expressed their own skepticism on this point. Thus Joan Didion in her essay "The Women's Movement": "That many women are victims of condescension and exploitation and sex-role stereotyping was scarcely news, but neither was it news that other women are not: nobody forces women to buy the package." De Beauvoir herself recognized that many members of her sex refuse to buy the "feminine" package: "The emancipated woman, on the contrary, wants to be active, a taker, and refuses the passivity man means to impose on her."

Since my college years, back in the murky 1960s, emancipated women have been discouraging their un-

emancipated sisters from making spectacles of themselves. Don't paint your face like a clown's or drape your
body like a mannequin's, they say. Don't bounce on the
sidelines in skimpy outfits, screaming your fool head off,
while men compete in the limelight for victories. Don't
present yourself to the world as a fluff pastry, delicate
and edible. Don't waddle across the stage in a bathing
suit in hopes of being named Miss This or That.

A great many women still ignore the exhortations.
Wherever a crown for beauty is to be handed out, many
still line up to stake their claims. Recently, Miss Indiana
Persimmon Festival was quoted in our newspaper about
the burdens of possessing the sort of looks that snag
men's eyes. "Most of the time I enjoy having guys stare
at me," she said, "but every once in a while it makes me
feel like a piece of meat." The news photograph showed
a cheerleader's perky face, heavily made-up, with
starched hair teased into a blond cumulus. She put me
in mind not of meat but of a plastic figurine, something
you might buy from a booth outside a shrine. Nobody
should ever be seen as meat, mere juicy stuff to satisfy
an appetite. Better to appear as a plastic figurine, which
is not meant for eating, and which is a gesture, however
crude, toward art. James Joyce described the aesthetic
response as a contemplation of form without the impulse
to action. Perhaps that is what Miss Indiana Persimmon
Festival wishes to inspire in those who look at her, perhaps that is what many women who paint and primp
themselves desire: to withdraw from the touch of hands
and dwell in the eye alone, to achieve the status of art.

By turning herself (or allowing herself to be turned)
into a work of art, does a woman truly escape men's pro-

prietary stare? Not often, says the British critic John Berger in *Ways of Seeing.* Summarizing the treatment of women in Western painting, he concludes that—with a few notable exceptions, such as works by Rubens and Rembrandt—the woman on canvas is a passive object displayed for the pleasure of the male viewer, especially for the owner of the painting, who is, by extension, owner of the woman herself. Berger concludes: "Men look at women. Women watch themselves being looked at. This determines not only most relations between men and women but also the relation of women to themselves. The surveyor of woman in herself is male: the surveyed female. Thus she turns herself into an object— and most particularly an object of vision: a sight."

That sweeping claim, like the one quoted earlier from De Beauvoir, also seems to me about three-quarters truth and one-quarter exaggeration. I know men who outdo the peacock for show, and I know women who are so fully possessed of themselves that they do not give a hang whether anybody notices them or not. The flamboyant gentlemen portrayed by Van Dyck are no less aware of being *seen* than are the languid ladies portrayed by Ingres. With or without clothes, both gentlemen and ladies may conceive of themselves as objects of vision, targets of envy or admiration or desire. Where they differ is in their potential for action: the men are caught in the midst of a decisive gesture or on the verge of making one; the women wait like fuel for someone else to strike a match.

I am not sure the abstract nudes favored in modern art are much of an advance over the inert and voluptuous ones of the old school. Think of two famous examples: Duchamp's *Nude Descending a Staircase* (1912), where the faceless woman has blurred into a waterfall of jagged shards, or Picasso's *Les Demoiselles d'Avignon* (1907), where the five angular damsels have been hammered as flat as cookie sheets and fitted with African masks. Neither painting invites us to behold a woman, but instead to behold what Picasso or Duchamp can make of one.

The naked women in Rubens, far from being passive, are gleefully active, exuberant, their sumptuous pink bodies like rain clouds or plump nebulae. "His nudes are the first ones that ever made me feel happy about my own body," a woman friend told me in one of the Rubens galleries of the Prado Museum. I do not imagine any pinup or store-window mannequin or bathing-suited Miss Whatsit could have made her feel that way. The naked women in Rembrandt, emerging from the bath or rising from bed, are so private, so cherished in the painter's gaze, that we as viewers see them not as sexual playthings but as loved persons. A man would do well to emulate that gaze.

I HAVE NEVER THOUGHT of myself as a sight. How much that has to do with being male and how much with having grown up on back roads where money was scarce and eyes were few, I cannot say. As a boy, apart from combing my hair when I was compelled to and regretting the patches on my jeans (only the poor wore patches), I took no trouble over my appearance. It never occurred to me that anybody outside my family, least of all a girl, would look at me twice. As a young man, when young women did occasionally glance my way, without any prospect of appearing handsome I tried at least to avoid appearing odd. A standard haircut and the cheapest versions of the standard clothes were camouflage enough. Now over the frontier of forty, I have achieved once more that boyhood condition of invisibility, with less hair to comb and fewer patches to humble me.

Many women clearly pass through the world aspiring to invisibility. Many others just as clearly aspire to be conspicuous. Women need not make spectacles of themselves in order to draw the attention of men. Indeed, for my taste, the less paint and fewer bangles the better. I am as helpless in the presence of subtle lures as a male moth catching a whiff of pheromones. I am a sucker for hair ribbons, a scarf at the throat, toes leaking from sandals, teeth bared in a smile. By contrast, I have always been more amused than attracted by the enameled exhibitionists whom our biblical mothers would identify as brazen hussies or painted Jezebels or, in the extreme cases, as whores of Babylon.

To encounter female exhibitionists in their full glory and variety, you need to go to a city. I never encountered ogling as a full-blown sport until I visited Rome, where bands of Italian men joined with gusto in appraising the charms of every passing female, and the passing females vied with one another in demonstrating their charms. In our own cities the most notorious bands of oglers tend to be construction gangs or street crews, men who spend much of their day leaning on the handles of shovels or pausing between bursts of riveting guns, their eyes tracing the curves of passersby. The first time my wife and kids and I drove into Boston we followed the signs to Chinatown, only to discover that Chinatown's miserably congested main street was undergoing repairs. That street also proved to be the city's home for X-rated cinemas and girlie shows and skin shops. LIVE SEX ACTS ON STAGE. PEEP SHOWS. PRIVATE BOOTHS. Caught in a traffic jam, we spent an hour listening to jackhammers and wolf whistles as we crept through the few blocks of pleasure palaces, my son and daughter with their noses out the windows, my wife and I steaming. Lighted marquees peppered by burnt-out bulbs announced the titles of sleazy flicks; life-size posters of naked women flanked the doorways of clubs; leggy strippers in miniskirts, the originals for some of the posters, smoked on the curb between numbers.

After we had finally emerged from the zone of eros, eight-year-old Jesse inquired, "What was *that* place all about?"

"Sex for sale," my wife Ruth explained.

That might carry us some way toward a definition of pornography: making flesh into a commodity, flaunting it like any other merchandise, divorcing bodies from selves. By this reckoning, there is a pornographic dimension to much advertising, where a charge of sex is added to products ranging from cars to shaving cream. In fact, the calculated imagery of advertising may be more harmful than the blatant imagery of the pleasure palaces, that frank raunchiness which Kate Millett refers to, in *Sexual Politics*, as the "truthful explicitness of pornography." One can leave the X-rated zone of the city, but one cannot escape the sticky reach of commerce, which summons girls to the high calling of cosmetic glamor, fashion, and sexual display, while it summons boys to the panting chase.

You can recognize pornography, according to D. H. Lawrence, "by the insult it offers, invariably, to sex, and to the human spirit" (from *Pornography and Obscenity*, a pamphlet he wrote amid the controversy surrounding *Lady Chatterley's Lover*). He should know, Millett argues in *Sexual Politics*, for in her view Lawrence himself was a purveyor of patriarchal and often sadistic pornography. I think she is correct about the worst of Lawrence, and that she identifies a misogynist streak in his work; but she ignores his career-long struggle to achieve a more public, tolerant vision of sexuality as an exchange between equals. Besides, his novels and stories all bear within themselves their own critiques. In *Language and Silence*, George Steiner reminds us that "the list of writers who have had the genius to enlarge our actual compass of sexual awareness, who have given the erotic play of the mind a novel focus, an area of recognition previously unknown or fallow, is very small." Lawrence belongs on that brief list. The chief insult to the human spirit is to deny it, to pretend that we are merely conglomerations of molecules, to pretend that we exist purely as bundles of appetites or as food for the appetites of others.

Men commit that insult toward women out of ignorance, but also out of dread. Allen Wheelis again, in *The Doctor of Desire*: "Men gather in pornographic shows, not to stimulate desire, as they may think, but to diminish fear. It is the nature of the show to reduce the woman, discard her individuality, her soul, make her into an object, thereby enabling the man to handle her with greater safety, to use her as a toy. . . . As women move increasingly toward equality, the felt danger to men increases, leading to an increase in pornography and, since there are some men whose fears cannot even so be stilled, to an increase also in violence against women."

Make her into an object: all the hurtful ways for men to look at women are variations on this betrayal. "Thus she turns herself into an object," writes Berger. A woman's ultimate degradation is in "submissively making herself a thing," writes De Beauvoir. To be turned into an object—whether by the brush of a painter or the lens of a photographer or the eye of a voyeur, whether by hunger or poverty or enslavement, by mugging or rape, bullets or bombs, by hatred, racism, car crashes, fires, or falls—is for each of us the deepest dread; and to reduce another person to an object is the primal wrong.

CAUGHT IN THE VORTEX of desire, we have to struggle to recall the wholeness of persons, including ourselves. In *The Second Sex,* De Beauvoir speaks of the temptation we all occasionally feel to give up the struggle for a self and lapse into the inertia of matter: "Along with the ethical urge of each individual to affirm his subjective existence, there is also the temptation to forgo liberty and become a thing." A woman in particular, given so much encouragement to lapse into thinghood, "is often very well pleased with her role as the *Other.*"

Yet one need not forgo liberty and become a thing, without a center or a self, in order to become the Other.

In our mutual strangeness, men and women can be doorways one for another, openings into the creative mystery that we share by virtue of our existence in the flesh. "To be sensual," James Baldwin writes in *The Fire Next Time,* "is to respect and rejoice in the force of life, of life itself, and to be *present* in all that one does, from the effort of loving to the breaking of bread." The effort of loving is reciprocal, not only in act but in desire, an *I* addressing a *Thou,* a meeting in that vivid presence. The distance a man stares across at a woman, or a woman at a man, is a gulf in the soul, out of which a voice cries, *Leap, leap.* One day all men may cease to look on themselves as prototypically human and on women as lesser miracles; women may cease to feel themselves the targets for desire; men and women both may come to realize that we are all mere flickerings in the universal fire; and then none of us, male or female, need give up humanity in order to become the Other.

Ever since I gawked at the girl in pink shorts, I have dwelt knowingly in the force field of sex. Knowingly or not, it is where we all dwell. Like the masses of planets and stars, our bodies curve the space around us. We transmit signals constantly, radio sources that never go off the air. We cannot help being centers of attraction and repulsion for one another. That is not all we are by a long shot, nor all we are capable of feeling, and yet, even after our much-needed revolution in sexual consciousness, the power of eros will still turn our heads and hearts. In a world without beauty pageants, there will still be beauty, however its definition may have changed. As long as men have eyes, they will gaze with yearning and confusion at women.

When I return to the street with the ancient legacy of longing coiled in my DNA, and the residues from a thousand generations of patriarchs silting my brain, I encounter women whose presence strikes me like a slap of wind in the face. I must prepare a gaze that is worthy of their splendor.

DUST

THE WORLD IS BEING GROUND TO BITS. DUST FROM THAT friction spirals in the sunlight before me, a galaxy of gleaming specks. With a steady fall that might sound, if amplified, like tribal drumming, dust settles onto the dark walnut surface of the table where I sit on our front porch. Night and day, indoors and out, the rain of infinitesimal debris never ceases. My family and I make our share by tracking dirt into the house, shredding lint from sheets and rugs and clothes, shedding hair and skin, nicking the woodwork, burning loaves by accident and logs on purpose. In the corners of hallways, beneath our beds and couches, behind our dressers, fluff gathers in wispy clouds. Through our windows the breeze delivers soil from plowed fields, soot from fires, ash from volcanoes, spew from cars and trucks, the spawn of bacteria, the spores of plants, the grit of meteors and quarries and mines, the down of birds, slivers of insects, scraps of whatever is broken, abraded, blown. Sitting here on the porch, warming my hands on a cup of tea, I swallow bits of world with every breath.

I am brooding about dust because my neighbor Malcolm and his family have just driven off to a nearby woods, where they will scatter the ashes of his mother, who died last week. Her name was Jane, this beaming, boisterous woman who shone like a lantern. I first encountered her several years ago, at a concert in the park. My wife and kids and I were chewing chicken and listening to the music when Jane crawled onto our blanket in pursuit of a roving grandchild. Age had whitened her hair and thickened her torso and charged her smile with a disarming radiance. She took a breather in our midst, inquiring about us between puffs. When she found out that we lived next door to her son, she told us gaily, "Oh, that Malcolm, he was a mistake. Born years and years after I thought I'd had my last child. He was a mistake, all right. Best one I ever made!" She laughed uproariously, proof that she had recovered breath. Excusing herself, she crawled off in search of the child. Her white hair flared among the darker heads of the crowd.

Had our meeting occurred a few years earlier, Malcolm tells me, Jane might have spun away from us doing cartwheels. She was famous among her offspring for handsprings, exuberant entrances and exits. As recently as a month ago, when she pulled up next door for a visit, her laugh still had the power to draw Malcolm's daughters out of the house to greet her as though she were an explorer newly returned from mysterious lands. She held out her hands to the bobbing girls and poured poetry over their heads. That was Jane. Today, the children help scatter her ashes, which by tomorrow may drift here to glint in the sunlight and sift into my lungs.

ASHES TO ASHES, dust to dust: the formula is easy to recite, hard to accept, especially when the ashes are those of someone who sang to us a week ago. Yorick, poor Yorick, whose songs and flashes of merriment were wont to set the table on a roar, has been reduced to the skull in Hamlet's hand. The loveliest lady will come to this, says Hamlet, no matter how thick she paints her face; the least and greatest will come to this, even world-conquering Alexander, whose "noble dust" might one day serve to stopper a beer-barrel.

We keep forgetting that dust is the common state, life the anomaly. One of Job's friends brags of God: "If he should take back his spirit to himself, and gather to himself his breath, all flesh would perish together, and man would return to dust." Our bodies are gatherings of earth, reared upright for a spell, replenished by food, water, air, and bound to sink again, soon. I lift a palm toward the sun, fingers pressed together, and red light burns through the cracks like the glow of lava through the fissures of a volcano. My fingertips turn fiery, incandescent. The nails are the rosy doors of furnaces. Despite the mind's reluctance, eyes insist that I am made from earth as literally as my tea mug is made from clay. Unless my clumsiness breaks it, the mug will outlast me, for it possesses the inertia of stone.

Much of our local dust began as stone. Topsoil in the hill country of southern Indiana consists chiefly of what geologists call loess, a silt that was scoured from bedrock by water and ice and was carried here by the wind eons ago. The layer beneath the loam is a ruddy clay stained red from iron, bearing the winsome name of terra rossa. Under the clay, only a few feet below our feet, is limestone, siltstone, sandstone. Our soil is the merest veneer on the round rock of the planet. The elm that fountains eighty feet in the air beside my front steps draws its huge nourishment from that thin crust, as do the daisies and tomatoes, the clover and grass, the ferns, the peonies, the phlox, as do my wife and children and I.

Without roots to stitch it together, the loam would blow away, as the soil of Texas and Oklahoma whirled away in the 1930s. You can hear the gritty wind howl in the songs of Woody Guthrie, who came of age in Oklahoma during those years. There is grit in his very titles: "Blowing Down this Old Dusty Road," "Dust Bowl Refugee," "Dust Pneumonia Blues," "Dust Storm Disaster." His "Talking Dust Bowl" opens with the lines:

Back in nineteen twenty-seven
I had a little farm and I called that heaven,
Well, the price was up and the rain came down,
And I hauled my crops all in to town.
  I got the money . . . bought clothes and groceries,
  Fed the kids and raised a family.
Rain quit and the wind got high,
And a black old dust storm filled the sky.

The towering black cloud approached his town, he recalled, like an elephant about to crush an ant. At midday the air became so dark you could not see the hand in front of your face. Neighbors gathered to comfort one another, certain the last judgment had arrived. They said quiet good-byes. There was no use, now, in wailing.

The Dust Bowl was an ecological judgment, if not a divine one. By turning over the prairie sod and planting dry land to row crops, farmers had created a desert. John Steinbeck describes the desolation in the opening chapter of *The Grapes of Wrath*:

When the night came again it was black night, for the stars could not pierce the dust to get down, and the window lights could not even spread beyond their own yards. Now the dust was evenly mixed with the air, an emulsion of dust and air. Houses were shut tight, and cloth wedged around doors and windows, but the dust came in so thinly that it could not be seen in the air, and it settled like pollen on the chairs and tables, on the dishes. The people brushed it from their shoulders. Little lines of dust lay at the door sills.

During the night the wind passed on. Farmers arose from sleep with a sense of dread: "In the morning the dust hung like fog, and the sun was as red as ripe new blood. All day the dust sifted down from the sky, and the next day it sifted down. An even blanket covered the earth. It settled on the corn, piled up on the tops of the fence posts, piled up on the wires; it settled on roofs, blanketed the weeds and trees."

DUST

In films of the Dust Bowl, the horizon disappears, land rises into the air, veil after veil of dirt unfurls. Those grainy, desolate scenes may provide a glimpse of how the world would look after nuclear war. Fewer people would die from blast and radiation, scientists now predict, than from hunger and cold, for explosions and fires would cloak the earth with soot, blocking the sun, killing the plants, chilling the air.

Scientists also speculate that something like that deep, enduring winter may have done in the dinosaurs, some sixty or seventy million years ago. The shroud of dust in that instance, according to a recent theory, was hurled into the atmosphere by the impact of a giant meteor. As evidence, geologists point to an ashy seam, rich in meteoric debris, that shows up widely in rock deposited about the time when the dinosaurs and most of their lumbering relatives expired. Ground to bits, to bits. Nothing will guarantee the survival of a species, if the largest creatures ever to walk the earth could be extinguished by dust.

ANGER, MAYHEM, CORRUPTION, and death lurk around the edges of the word. Our grandparents wrapped themselves in light coats called dusters when they toured in open automobiles, to protect their clothes. We wrap our hardcover books in dust jackets to protect the bindings (and to sell the contents). Dust ruffles form skirts around our beds, hiding the naked legs and enclosing a pasture for woolly flocks of lint. We sweep the day's leavings from our floors into dustpans. In England, the dustman empties your dustbin and hauls away your trash. Marx

69

predicted that workers would heave capitalism onto the dustheap of history.

An energetic person makes the dust fly. Servile, craven wretches lick the dust. A brawler gets in dustups and is forever dusting off opponents. Pitchers also dust off opponents, hurling the baseball at dangerous batters to worry them at the plate. We deceive someone by throwing dust in his eyes, in her eyes, a habit not so different from the notorious penchant of bullies for kicking sand in the faces of weaklings. A naughty child might well get his or her pants dusted. Eat my dust, says the boy in the schoolyard who thinks he owns the fastest feet. Desperadoes dust away from the scene of a crime. Bank robbers used to blow open vaults with sticks of dynamite they called, affectionately, sawdust.

Wheat dust, accumulating in grain elevators or the holds of ships, can explode. Crop dusters fly their noisy planes low over fields, spewing poison. As a boy, I knew we had reached Mississippi on our long drive from Ohio to visit my father's parents when I smelled the acrid poison of cotton dust. Buy our pickup, says the television ad, because Ford leaves Chevy in the dust, and the screen shows rival trucks tearing across the desert, the Chevy's plume lagging farther and farther behind. In the deserts of California and Nevada a century ago, the only dust worth mentioning was gold. Now, mention dust on a city street, and you are likely to be offered some powdered narcotic. Those who try the variety called angel dust, a synthetic heroin, often wind up crazy or dead.

To say that tough guys bite the dust may already have been a cliche by the time Homer used that expression—repeatedly—in the *Iliad*. Virgil used it again in the

Aeneid. Right up to our own day, writers of westerns have found it hard to kill off an Indian or an outlaw without resorting to that weary phrase. Eventually, we all bite the dust. But to see the job done properly, you need to study old cowboy movies. Shot through and through as he deserves, the villain spins and wobbles like a top in the parched street of a western town, wobbles and spins while delivering his last embittered lines, until his legs buckle and his heels kick up and his lips, his blasphemous lips, kiss the dirt.

I REHEARSE THE HARD LITANY—from ashes to ashes, dust to dust—while thinking of Malcolm's lovely, vanished mother. Every mother, if you think of her steadily enough, becomes your own. One of the first chores my mother assigned to me, when I was five or six, was dusting the furniture. I could never see the point of it. At that age, I could not see the point of taking a bath, either. Wood and skin, I reasoned, could hold only so much dirt; by cleaning, I was making way for more. Unpersuaded, Mother turned on the tap or handed me the rag. If I bathed before wiping the piano or the corner cupboard, then went outside to wrestle with the dog, by the time I came back in, the furniture and I would be freshly coated, thus proving my theory.

Without prompting now, for sheer pleasure, I go fetch the lemon oil and one of the children's old diapers, and I give the walnut table a good polishing. I relish the tangy smell of the oil. I love the gleam of the somber wood, its grain the current in a midnight river. Like all work, my rubbing imposes an order that is fleeting.

Soon, soon, after Jane's ashes have drifted here from the woods, after more grit from the abraded world has wafted in through our windows, I will be able to write with my finger in the table's gray film.

In my lifetime I have shaken enough dirt from vacuum cleaners to make a small moon. And still the carpets gather new fuzz. If I sweep the stairs, an hour later I find there a pale sprinkling, as though a light snow has fallen. Actual snow falls because ice crystals form around specks of dust, as do rain drops. Every flake, every drop carries down to us from high in the atmosphere a fleck of sky. Without dust the sunset would not be red; dusk would be the bleached, blank shade of noon.

THE WEEK OF JANE'S DEATH, the United States launched the Hubble Space Telescope, whose polished eye can detect the spark of a firefly ten thousand miles away. Each new generation of telescope has enabled us to see farther and farther into the universe, and what we continue to see, basically, is dust. Some of it is lumpy, forming stars and galaxies, but much of it is thinly scattered. Concentrations of interstellar dust, such as the Horsehead Nebula in Orion, appear to us by the darkness they carve out of the roof of light.

Stars are perennially casting off into space the atoms and molecules that will eventually form new suns, new earths. Some five billion years ago, our own sun and its necklace of planets coalesced out of drifting debris. The calcium in our bones, the iron in our blood, the carbon in the lead of the pencil with which I write these lines, all elements on earth much heavier than helium were formed in a previous generation of stars. That we are fashioned from the rubble of stars is a fact all the more appealing here in Bloomington, Indiana, where a local boy wrote the music for a song called "Star Dust."

> Though I dream in vain,
> In my heart it will remain—
> My stardust melody,
> The memory of love's refrain.

Hoagy Carmichael was crooning about romance, not cosmology. But love is only another attractive force, gathering self to self across the void. Even in dusty regions of space, astronomers calculate, on average each speck is separated from the next by the length of a football field. How such lonely motes could gather to form a lump, much less a galaxy, is a mystery we have labeled gravity. Mass yearns for mass. Longing stretches from end to end of the universe.

Whether the universe is open or closed we do not yet know. If it is closed, the galaxies that are now rushing apart will eventually slow down, snared by gravity, and will then come rushing back toward the center. If it is open, matter will expand outward forever, growing colder and colder, more and more dispersed, until atom loses track of atom.

JESUS INSTRUCTED HIS DISCIPLES to shake the dust from their feet before leaving a town where they had not been welcomed: "Truly, I say to you, it shall be more tolerable on the day of judgment for the land of Sodom and Gomorrah than for that town." His listeners knew that Sodom and Gomorrah—despite the arguments of Abraham, that man of dust and ashes—had suffered for their sins a rain of brimstone and fire, until "the smoke of the land went up like the smoke of a furnace." That line would be sobering to recall on any day in the last half of the twentieth century, a century in which the names of Dresden and Auschwitz and Hiroshima have come to stand for countless lives and lands gone up in smoke. It is a line all the more sobering to recall on a day so soon after the smoke of a friend's last burning has poured from the crematorium chimney.

EVENINGS AND WEEKENDS in childhood, the sound of the table saw or lathe would lure me to the basement, where my father was puttering. When I asked him what he was up to, one of his favorite responses was, "Making expensive sawdust." The air of the basement smelled ripe and sweet, as though the planks he cut were slabs of fruit. Actually, the sawdust that speckled my father's goggles and veiled the air cost little in money, for he was thrifty with wood and respectful of tools; but it was costly in time, for he would spend hours on a dovetail joint, days polishing a jewelry box, weeks inlaying a checkerboard with tiles of maple and cherry. Paraphrasing the Shakers, he told me that you should work as though you will live forever and as though you will die tomorrow.

For three years after his death, my father's ashes remained in their urn, wrapped in brown paper like a shameful purchase, tucked away on the top shelf of my mother's closet. All that while, she was deciding where

to scatter them, because my father, a man of this no-
madic century, had moved too many times to call any
place home. Eventually, we carried his ashes to Mississippi and strewed them over his parents' graves. I was
surprised to see, amid the gray powder, a few small nub-
bins of bone. I wanted to pick up one of those charred
scraps, pick up two or three, a handful, and stuff my
pockets. I wished to hold infinity in the palm of my
hand. I wished to seize time, squeeze the world, hold
on. But my mother stood beside me, grieving, and I only
stared down at the bright grass turned gray with ash. I
longed for rain, to erase the marks of our ceremony.

We are constantly being erased, our cells dying, and
we are constantly remade, molecule by molecule, some
parts of our bodies more swiftly, others more slowly.
With each renewal, we add mistakes, like photocopies
of photocopies growing ever fuzzier. Death is the final
blurring. Copied too many times, the likeness is lost.
The body forgets itself.

HERE ON THE LUMINOUS PORCH, with the sun blocked
out by my lifted palm, I can watch the motes in a shaft
of light jiggle and spin. The spectacle absorbs me no less
now than it did when I was a child. Already by the time
I was three or four, instead of taking a nap in the afternoon I would part the curtains to admit a crack of sun
and then lie there in the dark room, mesmerized by the
whirl of dust. If the air cleared, I would pound the pillow
or shake the quilt. I would puff to make the motes re-
volve.

As I grew older, my schools were too poor for telescopes and my eyes too poor for stargazing, so I gazed instead at specks and saw in them the cycling of worlds. Twenty-one centuries ago, Lucretius found in the whirl of dust, as he found in everything he observed, evidence that matter is compounded of atoms. He wrote of his perceptions early in the second book of *The Nature of Things* (translated here by Rolfe Humphries):

> *If you look sometimes,*
> *You see the motes all dancing, as the sun*
> *Streams through the shutters into a dark room.*
> *Look!—there they go, like armies in maneuver*
> *Whose little squadrons charge, retreat, join, part,*
> *From this you can deduce that on a scale*
> *Oh, infinitely smaller, beyond your sight,*
> *Similar turbulence whirls.*

The deeper we look into matter and the farther into space, the more clearly we see that Lucretius was right. On any scale, from the infinitesimal to the celestial, turbulence whirls.

After twenty-one hundred years, his conclusions hold up, but not his metaphors. I am glad to forgo the image of marching armies, because I have no use for armies. But I would like to say, with Lucretius, that the dust motes dance. I would like to stretch the metaphor, and speak of the hot, excited specks doing the tarantella, the warm ones doing the jitterbug or polka, the slow and stately ones doing the waltz. But to dance is to move in a pattern, driven by music. My sister and mother taught me to waltz by drawing a box on the kitchen linoleum and telling me to step from rose to rose. I shuffled around the edges of that box, left foot and right, one two three, one two three. From the waltz it was a hop and skip to the polka, the fox trot, the samba. I learned to square dance in the sweltering upper story of a village hall in Ohio, sawdust underfoot, a girl hooked to my elbow, the wail of fiddles and shouts of callers ringing in my ears. Fast or slow, the music worked through us; our bodies traced designs on the scuffed floor.

A passing knowledge of physics keeps me from saying that the dust motes dance, for they follow no music, obey no pattern. Their movement is an aimless jiggling, called Brownian motion after an English botanist named Robert Brown, who first described the effect with reference to pollen grains in water. Grains of anything, suspended in a liquid or gas, are buffeted by collisions with the surrounding atoms and molecules. That jostling is erratic, random, governed only by the size of the particles, the viscosity of the fluid, and the temperature. Translated into images on a screen, such motion produces scribbles, not the precise diagrams of a dance. Translated into sound, it produces not music but noise. Radio telescopes can still catch the muttering left over from the big bang that set our universe in motion some fifteen or twenty billion years ago. It is an inarticulate buzz, without syllables or syntax.

What is the deeper truth about this agitation of dust? Is it music or noise? And the shapes it takes on—Malcolm's mother, my hand, the splashing elm beyond the window, the pitted coin of the moon, the universe itself—have they been fashioned for a purpose, or are they

accidental shufflings of matter? Do the spheres dance, or
merely flounder? Our lives, our very lives, are they
speech or gibberish?

Like all the questions most worth asking, these are
ancient; we keep asking them because they admit no final answers. Though I have no way of proving it, I hold
by the view that our lives are not mere gibberish, but
are utterances of what we value, what we desire. Our
actions are the sum of what we mean. Like a car bumping down a dirt road, each of us leaves behind a faint
plume, a record of our passing. I also suspect, but am
even further from being able to prove, that Jane's laugh
and the veining in the elm's leaves and the fivefold
jointing of my hand are expressions, not of chance, but
of an inclusive order, an order that is more like the re-
sults of a mind thinking than like anything else I know.

RETURNED FROM SCATTERING his mother's ashes, Malcolm comes over to see me. We both feel the need to
dwell in our bodies, to labor and sweat, so we go out
back of my house with two spading forks to turn the fer-
menting compost in its wooden bin.

Soon our hearts are knocking from the work. Malcolm pauses for a moment to tell me that when he emptied the urn from a bluff on Clear Creek, he was surprised
to see most of the ashes tumble straight down instead of
wafting away. "They seemed heavy, the way they sank.
Heavy, instead of light."

I think of Jane's dust seeping into the bluff, to rise
next spring as bloodroot and larkspur, or washing into
the creek to become crayfish and water strider. "We see

the dancing motes in the sunlight," Lucretius wrote, "But we cannot see what urge compels the dancing." Here is a puzzle that should make us rise each day with questions on our tongue. The world is being ground to bits, yet the bits keep regathering to form the world anew.

II

PLACES

LANDSCAPE

AND

IMAGINATION

TO BE INTIMATE WITH A LANDSCAPE IS TO KNOW ITS moods and contours as you would know a lover's. The shape of breasts and hills, the sound of a laugh or the song of bullfrogs, the smell of hair and honeysuckle— such knowledge becomes part of who you are. As in marriage, however, what is utterly familiar may lose its charm, may in fact become invisible, until you are deprived of it. Absent yourself a while from lover or landscape, and upon returning you will recognize with fresh acuity what you had known but forgotten.

I experienced such a freshening of awareness not long ago, when I returned with my family to Indiana after a year's sojourn in Boston. We drove into the state one afternoon toward the end of July, the air rushing in our car windows like the breath from a furnace, a haze of muggy heat blurring the flat horizon. Thunderheads were massing in the west, grave clouds that cast their dark temper onto the whole countryside. A rising wind made silver maples show the pale undersides of their leaves and set cattails stirring in stock ponds and bent the trajectories of birds. After a year in the bunched-up terrain of New England, I was amazed by the extent of sky, the openness of the land, the vigor of the head-high corn, the loneliness of the farmsteads, the authority of those clouds.

We pulled over and shut off the engine for a change of drivers. I could smell hot tar bubbling in the joints of the road, creosote in telephone poles, windblown dust from cultivated fields, the mustiness of new-mown hay, the green pungency of Queen Anne's lace and chicory and black-eyed Susans. In the stillness I could hear the distant grumble of thunder like a clearing of throats, and the nearby ratcheting of crickets and cicadas. Only when I caught those smells, heard those sounds, did I realize how much I had missed them in the East, just as I had missed the sight of a level horizon broken by power lines, grain elevators, water towers, silos, and the shade trees around farmhouses. During our absence, the Midwest had suffered through a plague of cicadas. When we had called Indiana from Boston, the ruckus of insects over the telephone had all but drowned out the voices of our friends. Now, as I walked around to the passenger side of the car, cast-off cicada shells crunched under my feet. That sensation also was a re-discovery.

We angled south from Indianapolis toward home in Bloomington, coasting from the glacial plain into wooded hills, a landscape not so markedly different from that of New England. And yet even here my heightened senses picked up a flurry of details that characterize this place: limestone roadcuts, the white blaze of sycamores in creekbeds, pastures growing up in cedar and sumac, bottomlands planted in soybeans, sway-backed barns tattooed with ads for chewing tobacco, sinuous gravel driveways leading to basketball hoops, trailers and shacks interspersed with tidy ranch houses, the occasional white clapboard mansion encrusted with fretwork, the blither of billboards (outlawed in most of New England), the low-slung evangelical churches, and over it all that sovereign sky. The light was the silken yellow peculiar to a region of tornadoes. The fields recently harrowed were the color of buckskin. Unchecked by ocean or mountains, the storm that came roaring through the hills was another local species, its thunder jolting us inside the car with sudden changes in air pressure. In the twilight before the deluge, fireflies along the roadside blinked their semaphore of desire. Even in the dark that overtook us before we reached our front door, there was an unmistakable familiarity in the roasted-earth smell of rain and in the leap of lightning, which lit up the swirling treetops and shaggy hills.

THE EFFECTS OF MY YEAR away have not yet worn off. The landscape of the Midwest, familiar to me since childhood, still wears an air of novelty. T. S. Eliot spoke

of such a renewal of vision in those magisterial lines from
The Four Quartets:

> *We shall not cease from exploration*
> *And the end of all our exploring*
> *Will be to arrive where we started*
> *And know the place for the first time.*

It is increasingly rare for any of us to know with passion
and subtlety a particular place, whether a town or a state
or a region. We have itchy feet. Once every five years,
on average, we pull up stakes and move. No sooner do
we arrive somewhere than we begin hankering for a new
spot that's richer, more lively, more celebrated. Most of
the time we huddle indoors, gazing at magazine pages
and television screens that benumb us, no matter where
we live, with the same uprooted images. When we do
venture outside, we barrel along superhighways that
have been designed to ignore the terrain, past a blur of
franchise joints, or we glide through corridors above the
clouds.

Bothered by this, wishing to know the place where
I have been set down, I drive the back roads of Indiana,
tramp across country, wade the streams, look about. It
is never a simple matter actually to see what is before
your eyes. You notice what memory and knowledge and
imagination have prepared you to see. I take pleasure in
silos, for example—the antique masonry ones covered by
domed roofs, the squat silver ones wearing conical caps,
the giant blue steel ones bristling with chutes—partly
because their vertical strokes are a dramatic calligraphy
above the horizon, partly because, as a boy, I spent many

hours loading chopped cornstalks into the silo of a dairy farm and many hours more, half dizzy from the yeasty smell, pitching fermented silage to cows. As a teenager I also helped make hay and build houses, so there is beauty for me in a meadow of alfalfa freshly cut and raked into windrows, or a field humped with great round bales, or a pile of lumber beside a raw foundation, or the flash of a hammer in sunlight. My muscles know the ache and grace in such things. Likewise, for reasons of memory, I pay attention to all manner of barns, the venerable ones with boards missing as well as the brand spanking new ones. Admiring lone maples and oaks in pastures, their winter branches a net of nerves against the sky, their summer shade a haven for horses, I remember climbing such trees. Memory compels me to stop in the middle of railroad tracks and gaze down their latticed miles, to survey the junked cars and tractors and combines rusting in weed-grown ditches, to linger on the main streets of drowsy towns where clocks run slowly, to follow the inky flight of crows against a snow-covered hillside or the lope of a stray dog along a ridge. What I see is stitched through and through with my own past.

What I see when I look at the land is also informed by the company I have kept, beginning with that of my parents. Reared on a Mississippi farm, my father loved to poke about the countryside, studying crops and fences, eyeing the livestock. He would speculate on the quality of soil, squeezing a handful to judge the amount of clay, sniffing it, tasting a pinch. He wondered aloud about the facts of ownership and debt, since land took on meaning for him as property. A connoisseur of carpentry, he remarked with equal pleasure on weather-gray outhouses and gingerbread mansions. He counted the crossbars on telephone poles, by way of estimating the density of rural conversations. He would stop to shoot the breeze with idlers at gas stations and feed stores and doughnut cafes, wherever men with time on their hands gossiped about planting and harvest. He avoided cities, because little grew there aside from people, so much of the dirt had been paved, and because in cities he could not see, as he could on farms, the fruits of a family's or an individual's labor and skill. My father had little use for scenery. The land he cared for had been lived in, worked on, made over to fit human designs.

My mother, by contrast, is a city person with an artist's eye for texture and composition, and she goes to the country as to a feast for the senses. She notices every flower in bloom, the silhouettes of trees, the delicate tracery of hills, the architecture of clouds, the effects of light. What people have done to the land interests her less than what nature has done and is doing. My father's nose was ruined by smoking and boxing, but my mother more than makes up for it with a sense of smell that can detect lilacs or pigs from implausible distances. She can distinguish and name a hundred colors, many of them derived from oil paints, such as burnt sienna and raw umber. She can discern the slightest change in texture, as though the earth were a bolt of cloth over which she glides a subtle hand.

I learned what to notice and value in the landscape from both my parents, at first unconsciously and then deliberately. Like my mother, I exult in the nonstop show that nature puts on, the play of light and shade, the chorus of bird song and running water and wind-shaken trees, the seasons, the planet's voluptuous curves, and the infinite palette of paints. Like my father, I also relish the long-running human show, the fields cleared of stones, farmhouses built to capture sunlight and breezes, groves of walnuts planted as a legacy for grandchildren, high-tension lines, corncribs, orchards, bridges, anything that testifies to sweat and ingenuity and care. Between them, my parents taught me to honor whatever has been handsomely accomplished on the surface of the earth, whether by nature or by nature's offspring, us.

LIKE ALL LANDSCAPES, that of Indiana is a palimpsest, written over for centuries by humans and for millennia by the rest of nature. Every fence, highway, billboard, and clearing is an utterance, more or less eloquent, more or less durable. You can see, for example, in the checkerboard layout of crops and the right-angle turns of local roads the marks of a surveying grid that was imposed on all the country north and west of the Ohio River by the Land Ordinance of 1785. It was an unprecedented gesture, a Newtonian abstraction, reflecting the Enlightenment belief in reason, to ignore nature's own contours and inscribe on the land a uniform pattern of mile-square boxes. The map of the Midwest came to resemble graph paper, each block of which, in keeping with Jeffersonian ideals, was to support a citizen-farmer. The grid encouraged the establishment of isolated, self-sufficient homesteads, in contrast to the village culture of New England or the plantation culture of the South. During the period of settlement, what one did on his or her property was private business, and it remains largely private to this day, which is why zoning boards and planning commissions have such a hard time here, and why in many places the Indiana countryside is a hodgepodge of contradictory visions: grain fields alternating with strip mines, stretches of woods interrupted by used-car lots, dumps in ferny ravines, trailer courts in the middle of meadows, gas stations and motels plopped down wherever the traffic flows thickly enough. In much of Indiana, the isolated freeholdings have gradually been combined into larger and larger parcels, the remnants of forest have been cut down, the hedgerows cleared, the meandering creeks straightened, the swampy lowlands drained, thus further rationalizing the landscape, pushing it toward an industrial ideal of profitable uniformity.

Native creatures inscribe their own messages on the landscape, messages that one can learn, however imperfectly, to read. Deer trails mark out subtle changes in slope. The population of butterflies and owls and hawks is a measure of how much poison we have been using; the abundance of algae in ponds is a measure of our fertilizer use. The condition of trees is a gauge of the acidity in rain. Merely finding out the name and history of a plant may deepen one's awareness of a place. For years I had admired the coppery grass that grows in knee-high tufts along Indiana's roadsides before I discovered that it is called little bluestem, a survivor from the prairies. Now I admire those luminous grasses with new pleasure, for I see them as visitors from a wild past.

I also know from books that, except for dunes and prairies and swamps near Lake Michigan, all of what would become Indiana was dense with forest when the first white settlers arrived. This means that almost every acre of soybeans and corn represents an acre of trees cut down, stumps pulled out or left to rot: oak and beech, hickory and maple, dogwood, sassafras, buckeye, elm, tulip poplar, ash. In two centuries, a mere eyeblink in the long saga of the planet, Indiana has been transformed from a wilderness dotted by human clearings to a human landscape dotted by scraps of wilderness. Today, only the southern third of Indiana is heavily wooded, but the speed with which redbud and locust and cedars march into abandoned pastures convinces me that the entire state, left to itself, would slip back into forest again within a few decades. The highways, untraveled, would succumb to grass. The barns and houses, unroofed, would succumb to rain. It does not trouble me to see our clearings as ephemeral, our constructions as perishable, for that is the fate of all human writing, whether on paper or on earth.

Despite our centuries of scrawling on the landscape, we can still read the deeper marks left by nature—especially, in Indiana, the work of water and ice. For millions of years, while the Appalachians were being uplifted to the east and the Rockies to the west, the land that would become Indiana was forming grain by grain in the bed of an ancient ocean, as limestone, siltstone, sandstone, dolomite, shale, slate. It was and remains a placid region, at the core of the continental plate. These sedimentary rocks have never been folded, never heaved up into mountains nor deeply buried and cooked into granite or marble, never burst open by volcanoes. When the waters receded, the bedrock, exposed to wind and rain, was carved into low hills. Beginning roughly a million years ago and ending some ten thousand years ago, glaciers bulldozed down from the north, flattening the hills and filling the valleys and burying much of the Midwest beneath a fertile layer of dust and pulverized rock. In their retreat, the glaciers gouged out the stony bed of the Great Lakes and filled them with water, altered the flow of rivers, and left behind a trail of gravel and sand. In Indiana, only a thumb-shaped area stretching about a hundred miles north from the Ohio River escaped the glaciers. The limestone exposed there is laced with caves and underground rivers, pockmarked by sinkholes. Knowing even this much geological history, I look at the flat expanses of black loam, or the polished quartz in a creekbed, or the strata of shale in a bluff with a chastening sense of nature's slow rhythms and our hasty ones.

WITHOUT THESE LESSONS in seeing, from people and memories and books, I might view the landscape before me as little more than a straggle of postcards. In fact, without benefit of instruction, in a territory as unglamorous as the Midwest I might fail to appreciate even the two-dimensional postcard views. Of all the regions in America, this one has inspired, I would guess, the least smugness from local people and the least rapture from travelers. People do not move here for the scenery. They do not commonly even visit here for the scenery. I have no way of checking, but I would venture that fewer landscape snapshots are taken per square mile in the Midwest than in any other part of the country, including the deserts. Millions of people drive through Indiana every year without lifting their gaze from the highway. Those who do glance aside from the line of motion tend to see only indistinguishable fields and humble hills.

I have spent enough time in the mountains of Oregon and Tennessee, the redwood forests of California, the mesa country of New Mexico, the moss-festooned bayous of Louisiana, and along the stony coast of Maine to know the pleasures of spectacular landscapes. How could anyone equipped with nerves fail to rejoice in such places? On the other hand, to know the pleasures of an unspectacular landscape, such as that of Indiana, requires an uncommon degree of attentiveness and insight. It requires one to open wide all the doors of perception. It demands an effort of imagination, by which I mean not what the Romantics meant, a projection of the self onto the world, but rather a seeing of what is already there, in the actual world. I don't claim to possess the necessary wisdom or subtlety, but I aspire to, and I work at it.

Wherever we live in America, many of those who preceded us were so bent on changing the land to suit their needs that they scarcely looked at what was native. We have only recently begun to realize how much was lost in that refusal to look. Those who preceded us here found an astonishing wealth, not only in lumber and loam and oil, but in the intricacy and beauty of life. Yet they valued almost exclusively what could be used or sold. Generations of settlers treated the land as a storehouse, to be ransacked before moving on. The fact that we dislodged Indians from their home grounds and herded them onto reservations a thousand miles away

reveals how little our ancestors valued the sacred connection between a people and a landscape. We are still
suffering from the Puritan habit of regarding wild nature
as demonic, a realm to be conquered and saved from the
Devil. The secular version of this view treats land as raw
material for profit; whatever does not yield a return in
dollars stands in need of "development," which is an
economic form of salvation. Thus a chorus of angry
voices cries down every proposal for the creation of wilderness areas or the preservation of wetlands or even for
restrictions on the clear-cutting of trees.

Insofar as we are nomads, adrift over the earth and
oblivious to its rhythms, we cease to acknowledge the
fecund mystery that sustains our existence. We take in-
ordinate pride in our own doings. Acting without regard
for the effects our lives will have upon a place, we become dangerous, to ourselves and our descendants. If our
own senses fail to teach us, then disasters will, that the
land is not merely a backdrop for the human play, not
merely a source of raw materials, but is the living skin
of the earth. Through this skin we apprehend a being
that is alien, a life unfathomable and uncontrollable,
and at the same time a being that is kindred, flesh of
our flesh.

It is a spiritual discipline to root the mind in a particular landscape, to know it not as a visitor with a camera but as a resident, as one more local creature alongside
the red-tailed hawks and sycamores and raccoons. The
explorations from which we return to see our home
ground afresh may be physical ones, such as my family's
sojourn in New England, or they may be journeys of the

mind, such as those we take through stories and photographs and paintings. By renewing our vision of the land, we rediscover where it is we truly dwell. Whatever the place we inhabit, we must invest ourselves there with our full powers of awareness if we are to live responsibly, alertly, wisely.

LOCAL

MATTERS

IN ANCIENT JAPAN, YOU REALIZED YOU HAD WANDERED from your neighborhood when you could no longer hear the sacred drum. I know I've left my neighborhood when I can no longer hear the infernal dogs. Fenced up in backyards or chained to front porches, with only time on their paws, they devote themselves to barking. They protest the arrivals and celebrate the departures of milkman, mailwoman, butcher, baker, grocer, plumber, joggers, bicyclists, every soul that ventures down our street. They howl at ambulances and airplanes. They growl at school children. They bark at invisible, perhaps even metaphysical, provocations. No opera singer is more diligent at running the scales of outrage and grief.

I open with dogs, because their racket this morning has kept me from thinking of much else. I don't mean to complain. Far better a few noisy mutts outside than muggers or pushers or soldiers cradling machine guns. I realize that dogs bark on other streets, in other towns, indeed in every state of this pet-mad nation. You may well be grimacing at a mongrel's yap even as you read this. Distant dogs I can ignore, just as I ignore the faults of strangers and the leaks in other people's roofs. But these are my *local* dogs, whose voices therefore penetrate through windows and walls to skewer my brain.

Their owners, indulgent or deaf, suffer them to bark. What should I do? My American upbringing offers three alternatives: kill the brutes, sue the owners, or move house. I am tempted by all three, but instead I shove in earplugs and grit my teeth. Why? Setting aside my character flaws—a sympathy for captives and a dislike of quarrels, to name only a pair—I put up with the ruckus because the dogs and their owners, along with ancient sewers and modern chuckholes, belong to my neighborhood, just as I do. I am convinced that you marry a place, if you truly want to live there, as you marry a spouse, for better or for worse. Having to listen to the bellow of dogs is a small tax to pay for the privilege of living in a community.

It *is* a privilege these days, and a rarity, to live as my wife and kids and I do in a dumpy old house surrounded by a leafy yard, within a five-minute walk of our jobs, within shouting distance of several dozen friends, close to parents and forests and theaters and a library holding millions of books. Except in the coldest weather, you can always find somebody in the street—kids lobbing tennis balls against limestone walls, heart patients out for a saunter, couples wheeling drowsy babies, idlers primed for talk. In our neighborhood, cats turn up on the front steps, squirrels at the back. Swifts dart in and out of chimneys. Our yards are crowded with swing-sets, bird feeders, compost heaps, and flowers that can tolerate the shade of elderly maples and elms and oaks. We lug our banjos and babies into one another's living rooms and make music. We eat in one another's kitchens. On many an evening, you can see us carrying salads and casseroles and hot loaves of bread up and down the street. We do not often think to lock our doors.

I am never more aware of how fully I belong to this neighborhood and this region than when I return to it after a sojourn elsewhere, as I have just returned with my family after a year away. Nothing we heard about Indiana over the official channels during our stay in Boston would have encouraged us to come back. We did not hear much. National television crews never passed anywhere near this place, so far as we could tell. Newspapers and radio told us that Indiana had suffered a locust infestation and an earthquake, that a Hoosier boy afflicted with AIDS had been turned away from school, that Indiana law permits capital punishment of children, and that a southern Indiana drive-in was shutting its gates for lack of customers. The longest report of all concerned a flock of plastic flamingos that disappeared from a Hoosier yard on Memorial Day and reappeared, gussied up in tuxedos and tutus, on Labor Day. From these items one formed a vision of Indiana as a land forgotten by time, where vengeful wackos and raw nature still hold sway.

In spite of that discouraging news, we came back here anyhow. These homecomings are a habit with us. My wife, Ruth, and I have spent seven of the past twenty years living elsewhere—in England, New Hampshire, Oregon, Massachusetts—and each time, like salmon nosing our way back to ancestral waters, we have returned to this town. For the past decade and a half we have returned to the same creaky old house, first with one child and then with two.

Acquaintances who live on the coast or in one of the inland metropolises where you can buy, say, Armenian shish kebab at three in the morning, wonder aloud how we can withdraw to such a backwater. They imagine our town is Our Town, or Middletown, or Spoon River, or Winesburg, or Gopher Prairie, or some other stifling burg where teetotalers bang courting youngsters over the head with umbrellas and doomsayers rant on the only street corner. The place is not so remote as it may appear through metropolitan telescopes, however. If anything, it is not isolated *enough* for my taste. The town has cable television, which means we can see pretty much what everyone else can see. Our bookstores carry the best and worst of what there is to read, our cinemas show the latest movies, our auditoriums and bars host performers from all over the map. You can get the day's *New York Times*, *Chicago Tribune*, and *Wall Street Journal* delivered to your front door each morning, should you have nothing better to do with your time. And if you get bored with the restaurants or museums, within an hour or two you can fly to any of a dozen cities that rank high in the census.

It's harder and harder to find a true backwater. In a durable essay called "The Long-Legged House," Wendell Berry, farmer and poet, makes the point about his own seemingly remote corner of Kentucky: "Here as well as anywhere I can look out my window and see the world. There are lights that arrive here from deep in the universe. A man can be provincial only by being blind and deaf to his province." All points on the map are lit by a single juice. The earth is never likely to become a global village, if only because in a true village every citizen is wrapped in a mesh of gossip and concern; but, increasingly, all our settlements are stitched together by the neurons of transport and communication, until the same products cross our shelves, the same foods cross our tables, the same images cross our minds. I could do with more isolation.

Still, it is a fair question those big-city acquaintances ask me. I have often wondered myself—especially in Boston, where I heard the siren songs of high culture, smelled the salt sea, dodged limousines that were bearing movers and shakers to historic appointments—what draws me back to this place. Filthy lucre is a factor, of course: I have a job here. But there were jobs galore in Boston. My skills, such as they are, are portable. I could make a go of it elsewhere. The tug of friendship and neighborhood is far stronger, for me, than money. I come back here because, when I look out my window, I feel a connection to all that I see, even to those blasted dogs.

No matter where one lives, there's always someplace else more glamorous, with more nightspots to visit, more dollars to grab, more glittery names to drop. Part of me hankers to try new places, new jobs, new dogs; to light out for the Territory, head for the mountains or the metropolis. I wouldn't be a born-and-bred American if I didn't feel that hankering. Which is not to say that Americans invented mobility. If there weren't a wanderlust in our whole species, all of humanity would still be camped in our aboriginal valley in Africa. But we Americans do have some of the itchiest feet in history. Motion comes naturally to us. We brag about the number of places we've lived. We look with suspicion or scorn at people who stay put.

It is rare for any of us, by deliberate choice, to sit still and weave ourselves into a place, so that we know the wildflowers and rocks and politicians, so that we recognize faces wherever we turn, so that we feel a bond with everything in sight. The challenge, these days, is to be *somewhere* as opposed to nowhere, actually to belong to some particular place, invest oneself in it, draw strength and courage from it, to dwell not simply in a career or a bank account but in a community.

Once you commit yourself to a place, you begin to share responsibility for what happens there. When PCBs leak into the water or dioxides into the air, it is your water and your air that is polluted. The parks, the schools, the hospitals, the government, all are yours to fret over. When kids knock at your door, requesting donations for the band or the debate team or the purchase of a limestone rhinoceros, you have to reach for your wallet. Entangle yourself in a place, and you become attached to your neighbors as to kinfolk. When some of them pull up stakes and leave, as friends from down the street have just done—to Washington, D.C., where the husband will work at the Smithsonian, the wife will teach Spanish, and the two daughters will sprout into mysterious teenagers—you grieve. If a local woman is raped, a child goes hungry, a man is denied a job because of the shade of his skin, you are implicated. You must answer to the needs of a community, and if you neglect those needs, as I too often do, slipping back into the hammock of private life, you eat the sour bread of guilt.

No wonder our songs tell us we gotta keep travelin' on. Who needs to shoulder the weight of a community when our own skins weigh so heavily? The impulse to hit the road is not only a hunger for new territory; it is often a flight from trouble. Daniel Boone is famous for having moved on whenever he could see the smoke from a neighbor's fire. Many of us move on to avoid cleaning up the ashes from the fires we ourselves have set.

Local matters; the local matters. We shouldn't take too narrow a view of the neighborhood. Astronomers speak of the Milky Way and a few nearby galaxies as the "local cluster." Remember how Thoreau, nagged by his friends to venture out and see the world, replied that he had no need of such journeying, for he had already traveled extensively in Concord. My feet are itchier than Thoreau's, my character is muddier. Hit the road if you're so inclined, I say, and explore distant parts. But then go home again. Pick your own Concord, and travel there. If your eyes are open, you'll see more than you have brain for.

In the warmer months, during a lull in the concert of motorcycles and locusts, I sometimes hear heavy breathing from the sky and look up to see a hot-air balloon drifting over, its burner snorting, its passengers gazing down like gods. I imagine that from their lofty perspective they see this neighborhood the way I experience it, as a web of streets and gardens and lives. If a whole fleet of balloons were to sail over now, I'd never hear them through the barking. As soon as Ruth comes home from the lab, where she has been wrestling with rats for the good of science, I'll see if she won't go out there and deal with those dogs.

SIGNS

WE SEEM COMPELLED TO SCRAWL OUR WORDS ON THE
mute, impervious world. We label the trees in parks, the
caged animals in zoos. We encumber the horizon with
billboards. We paste wisdom and wisecracks on the
bumpers of cars, wear messages on our T-shirts, leave
notes on refrigerators. In hospitals we hang names on
the cribs of newborns, and in cemeteries we carve names
above the dead. Watch any bare wall or lamppost, and
before long it will blossom with signs, posters, the ini-
tials of lovers. Look at any map, and see how names
crowd the blank spaces.

   If you get out the road atlas and flip to the map of
Indiana, say, and if you let your finger spiral toward my
burg of Bloomington in the southern part of the state,

you will trace over Gnaw Bone, Possum Trot, Buddha, Tulip, Handy, Pinhook, Peerless, Hope and New Hope, Beanblossom, Piano, Mount Healthy, Story, and Surprise. Wide places in the road, mostly, but they all carry labels, as do the creeks, the bridges, the government forests, the roads themselves.

Say you fly to Indianapolis, rent a car, drive south on Route 37, a four-lane that bears the name of a dead highway commissioner. After an hour of housing tracts and soybean fields and rumpled woodlands, you approach Bloomington through the gauntlet of hectoring signs that ring most American cities, billboards urging you to smoke this brand of cigarette, drink that whiskey, sleep in this motel, drive that car, buy and buy, eat, eat, eat. You have been called into the world to devour it, the billboards cry. None of this is local speech. These garish ads for national brands are like distant voices hurled at us through loudspeakers; they are slabs of network culture heaved up on stilts and frozen against the sky. But if you leave the highway and enter the city, you pass through layer after layer of signs, each one more local and quirky than the one before, until, on reaching the downtown alleys, you find painted on brick walls the slogans and hieroglyphs of this particular place.

Turn off the highway, then. Take the College Avenue exit. Cruise past the billboards for lawyers, realtors, restaurants, banks. Check out the titles of this week's teenybopper movies playing at the Y & W drive-in. Slow down. Notice in yards the hand-lettered rectangles of plywood and cardboard and tin, signs offering to pull stumps, read palms, figure taxes, clean septic tanks, upholster chairs, weave rugs, sell porch swings and quilts.

You can almost hear the seethe of enterprise. On more official signs, twenty flavors of churches invite you to worship. Service clubs—Moose, Lions, Elk, the whole menagerie—invite you to lunch. Funeral homes invite you to think ahead. Tune us in, beg the radio stations. Read us, beg the newspapers. Remember us, beg the charities. The air is filled with seductive babble.

Where woods give way to the spreading hem of houses, the city greets you with a sign for the Cascades Softball Complex (which sounds engagingly Freudian), and then, because every crossroads aspires to be the center of *something*, Bloomington introduces itself as the Home of the Children's Organ Transplant Association. All over town you will see C.O.T.A. fund-raising banners, from which bald infants in need of livers or kidneys gaze at you hopefully.

You reach the outermost traffic light. On your right is the first of three Big Red Liquor stores you will pass within two minutes. Go straight on College Avenue, which runs along one flank of the courthouse square. A mile from the square, the round sign of the Big Wheel Restaurant flashes in sequence its neon spokes, creating the illusion of a spinning wheel. The electronic marquee of a savings & loan spells out the time, temperature, interest rates, and news about the Girl Scout cookie sale. A mural on the second Big Red Liquor shows the Hoosier hills in autumn, scarlet maple and golden poplar. Drink, drink, and be mellow. On slotted plastic signs that shoulder for space along the avenue, a car dealer pleads "Come on Rain," Fantasy Lingerie offers "Adult Models," a pizza palace boasts "No Fooling, We're Number One," a burger joint confesses "We've Never Sold

Millions of Anything," and a gas station promises, with spelling that gives one pause, "Mechantic on Duty."

Four blocks from the courthouse, a cartoon sign above Custom Grooming shows a cheerful woman with curly blond hair and ruby lips, the fingers of one uplifted hand signaling V-for-Victory, the other hand grasping the leash of a beige poodle. You cannot tell without going inside that the grooming is for dogs, not women. Pleazure Hours Adult Bookstore beckons from the right, across the street from Big Red Liquor number three. Even on so brief an acquaintance with our city, you realize that no one possessed of cash need go hungry or lonely or dry.

Pull into one of the angled spaces beside the courthouse and park. Get out and stretch. You might puzzle at seeing a copper fish atop the courthouse dome. Everybody does, but no one can say for sure why an aquatic weathervane presides over this town so far from the sea. On the courthouse lawn, next to the Women's Christian Temperance Union fountain ("Drink and Be Grateful"), a plywood sheet braced with two-by-fours marks the "Future Site of Vietnam Veterans Memorial." It has been a future site for so long, the donations accumulating so sluggishly, that the wood has begun to warp, the paint to peel. Awaiting their memorial, the veterans do not let the war end, for their sign shows a map of Vietnam still sharply divided between north and south, the north stained a demonic red and the south a tranquil green.

Milder struggles are played out in the downtown's welter of signs and countersigns. Take an hour, walk the streets and alleys within two or three blocks of the courthouse, and you will see other traces of embattled visions.

To begin with, head west from the square along Sixth, past the Ben Franklin five-and-dime. Halfway down the block you come to the dingy office of Yellow Cab, on whose roof there is a billboard-size imitation of Leonardo's "Last Supper," done in splotches of bright primary colors like a gigantic paint-by-numbers project. On a traffic signal box out front of Yellow Cab, someone has written "Trust Jesus," and above this injunction another hand has written "Don't."

A mural of the holy supper comes as no surprise here, for Bloomington is a notch in the Bible belt, the seat of a county whose barns and silos are apt to proclaim "Get Right with God!" or "Jesus Is Lord!" But the contrary impulse, the mocking voice that adds "Don't" before "Trust Jesus," is also native to the place. On bridges and underpasses and in the shadows of alleys, where the devout have scrawled "He Is Risen" or "He Is Coming," ribald skeptics draw erupting phalluses. "Jesus Saves" is amended with the words, "in His Piggy Bank." Wags repeatedly steal the "S" from the SHELL signs. Adherents of a more furtive faith chalk up notices that "Good Witchcraft Is Alive." Walk another half block past the paint-by-numbers Leonardo and, within sight of two churches, you will discover on the back of a grocery store the warning, "Don't Love Gods!"

In your stroll around the square, time and again you will see this pattern, an official vision fronting the street and a rebel vision flickering in the alley. Behind the fattest of our several fat banks, critics have spray-painted "Lance That Boil" and "Pride Kills." On the front of the Knights of Columbus building, this month's antiabortion broadside proclaims "Always Choose Life," while on the rear someone has written in small, fierce letters, "Choose Choice!" A downtown cinema known for running the more witless breed of movies has been inscribed with "Post No Dreams" and "100% Unconscious by the Year 2000." A record store has inspired the milder and wittier protest, "I'm Not Your Groovy Thing!" When a grassy vacant lot—favorite hang-out for skateboarders and singers and Frisbee flingers—vanished recently under a new gimcrack store, the fresh paint on the alley was soon emblazoned with "Town for Sale!"

Stick to the alleys and you begin to see clashes, not only between official and rebel visions, but among the dissidents themselves. "Kill Art!" appears behind Pygmalion's Art Supplies, but so does the rival claim that "Artists Control the Means of Expression!" A pastel mural of frolicking citizens has been smirched with paintings of houseflies the size and color of crows. Behind Bloomingfood's vegetarian co-op, a carnivore has painted "Raw Meat!" in bloody tones, but a gentler spirit has replied with "Love All Beings, Only Life Is Holy." Elsewhere, the call to "Stop CIA Terrorism" is answered by "Off the Gooks," and the rare, nostalgic peace symbol is answered by a swastika.

Despite the efforts at cheer, the dominant tone in the alleys is grim, reflecting the histrionic postures but also the confusion and despair of the young people who paint most of the graffiti. The skull and crossbones is a common motif, often accompanied by "Shatter Yourself" or "Life Sucks." Keep walking, and you read: "Give me drugs!" "Born to lose!" "It just doesn't matter!" "Can't wait to be extinct!" The stenciled silhouettes of women, headless and ghostly white, cling to the brick walls like the shadows of pedestrians cast by the nuclear flash onto the walls of Hiroshima. The blunt four-letter word for lovemaking appears frequently, but more as curse than exhortation. "Sex = Death" appears on the back of Nick's English Hut, written by a metaphysician who was perhaps frightened by AIDS, perhaps moved by intimations of the link between loving the flesh and leaving it. The voices are local, but they speak of universal things.

In the alleys, on the cindery edges of parking lots, in the gloomy back passageways, tokens of hope never go unchallenged. On a mailbox near the Lutheran Church a moving hand has written "Just Believe," but another has countered with "Big Daddy in the Sky's a Bum!" Rosy letters cry "Love Now!" from the delivery door of a boutique, and black ones answer:

> *It's not allowed to be unkind,*
> *But still hate lives in my mind.*

That is bleak enough, and yet, in such strangled poetry, in puns and rhymes, in outbursts of wackiness and whimsy, the alleys offer an antidote to their own bitter messages. Here and there on the gray cement a mushroom cloud has been redrawn into the humped shell of a snail, above the caption, "Slugs are friends." The score of a composition for brass quintet marches across the wall of a music store in notes a yard high. Sidewalks and dumpsters are embellished with a simple visual pun:

MOM
WOW

A rental house is labeled "Roach Motel." The windows of apartments over shops bear the warnings "Guard Snake on Duty" or "Beware of Canary." Next to dreary mottoes of ennui, you find the fluttering peacock-bright posters for dances, concerts, revivals, lessons in meditation, motorcycles for sale, kittens for free. Amid the gloomy pronouncements about sex, you read the perennial news that "Fred loves Nancy," Jack loves Jill.

The alleys become our caves. We paint on their walls the symbols of what we love and hate, what we fear and worship, what we hunt and what we feel ourselves hunted by. With pictures, poems, and slogans, we gesture at mysteries. Like the cave artists who traced the outlines of their hands on the ceiling of Lascaux, we leave marks that say of us: Here I am, the one who sees, the one who shapes. The power of naming our grief gives us leverage over despair, the power of voicing our confusion gives us a grip on chaos. Another couplet sums up the equivocal mood of the alleys:

> *I opened my mouth to vomit,*
> *But all I got were words.*

At least it is an individual mouth, not the great maw of a corporation or an advertising firm. And at least, against the silence, words do come. Words, the outbreathings of mind, the shadows cast by inwardness: they cover the walls of my city, and no doubt of yours, they blot out chunks of sky, they make the unspoken world speakable.

When your eyes grow weary of symbols or your feet

of pavement, look for the copper fish gliding atop the courthouse dome, and make your way back to the car. To leave Bloomington, hang two lefts around the square, then take Walnut north to 37, from which you can easily retrace your path to the airport. Signs will shout and whisper at you all the way.

GRUB

THE MORNING PAPER INFORMS ME THAT, ONCE AGAIN this year, Indiana leads the nation in fat. The announcement from the Centers for Disease Control puts it less bluntly, declaring that our state has "the highest percentage of overweight residents." But it comes down to the same thing: on a globe where hunger is the rule, surfeit the exception, Indiana is first in fat.

I read this news on Saturday morning at a booth in Ladyman's Cafe, a one-story box of pine and brick wedged between the Christian Science Reading Room and Bloomington Shoe Repair, half a block from the town square. It is a tick after 6:00 A.M. My fellow breakfasters include a company of polo-shirted Gideons clutching Bibles, a housepainter whose white trousers are speckled with the colors of past jobs, two mechanics in overalls with *Lee* and *Roy* stitched on their breast pockets, three elderly couples exchanging the glazed stares of insomniacs, and a young woman in fringed leather vest and sunglasses who is browsing through a copy of *Cosmopolitan.* Except for the young woman and me, everyone here is a solid contributor to Indiana's lead in fat. And I could easily add my weight to the crowd, needing only to give in for a few weeks to my clamorous appetite.

I check my belt, which is buckled at the fourth notch. Thirty-two inches and holding. But there are signs of wear on the third and second and first notches, tokens of earlier expansions.

The lone waitress bustles to my booth. "Whatcha need, hon?" Her permed hair is a mat of curls the color of pearls. Stout as a stevedore, purple under the eyes, puckered in the mouth, she is that indefinite age my grandmother remained for the last twenty years of her long life.

"What's good today?" I ask her.

"It's all good, same as every day." She tugs a pencil from her perm, drums ringed fingers on the order pad. Miles to go before she sleeps. "So what'll it be, sugar?"

I glance at the smudgy list on the chalkboard over the counter. Tempted by the biscuits with sausage gravy, by the triple stack of hotcakes slathered in butter, by the twin pork chops with hash browns, by the coconut cream pie and glazed doughnuts, I content myself with a cheese omelet and toast.

"Back in two shakes," says the waitress. When she

charges away, a violet bow among her curls swings into
view, the cheeriest thing I have seen so far this morning.

I buy breakfast only when I'm on the road or feeling
sorry for myself. Today—abandoned for the weekend by
my wife and kids, an inch of water in my basement from
last night's rain, the car hitting on three cylinders—I'm
feeling sorry for myself. I pick Ladyman's not for the
food, which is indifferent, but for the atmosphere, which
is tacky in a timeless way. It reminds me of the truck
stops and railroad-car diners and jukebox cafes where my
father would stop on our fishing trips thirty years ago.
The first thing you see, on entering, is a cigarette vend-
ing machine at the end of the counter, as though the
folly of smoking were still a secret here. The oilcloth that
covers the scratched Formica of the table is riddled with
burns. The Naugahyde seat of my booth has lost its stuff-
ing, broken down by a succession of hefty eaters. The
walls, sheathed in vinyl for easy scrubbing, are hung
with fifty-dollar oil paintings of covered bridges, pastures, and tree-lined creeks. The floor's scuffed linoleum
reveals the ghostly print of deeper layers, material for
some future historian of cafes. Ceiling fans turn overhead, stirring with each lazy spin the odor of tobacco
and coffee and grease.

There is nothing on the menu of Ladyman's that was
not on the menus I remember from those childhood fishing trips. But I can no longer order from it with a child's
obliviousness. What can I eat without pangs of unease,
knowing better? Not the eggs, high in cholesterol, not
the hash browns, fried in oil, not the fatty sausage or
bacon or ham, not the salty pancakes made with white

flour nor the saltier biscuits and gravy, not the lemon meringue pies in the glass case, not the doughnuts glistering with sugar, not the butter, not the whole milk.

Sipping coffee (another danger) and waiting for my consolatory breakfast, I read the fine print in the article on obesity. I learn that only thirty-two states took part in the study. Why did the other eighteen refuse? Are they embarrassed? Are they afraid their images would suffer, afraid that tourists, knowing the truth, would cross their borders without risking a meal? I learn that Indiana is actually tied for first place with Wisconsin, at 25.7 percent overweight, so we share the honors. For Wisconsin, you think of dairies, arctic winters, hibernation. But Indiana? We're leaders in popcorn. Our hot and humid summers punish even the skinny, and torture the plump. Why us? There's no comment from the Indiana Health Commissioner. This gentleman, Mr. Woodrow Myers, Jr., who weighed over three hundred pounds at the time of his appointment, lost a hundred pounds in an effort to set a healthy example, but has now gained most of them back. He doesn't have much room to talk.

My platter arrives, the waitress pausing only long enough to murmur, "Eat up, hon," before she hustles away. The omelet has been made with processed cheese, anemic and slithery. The toast is of white bread that clots on my tongue. The strawberry jelly is the color and consistency of gum erasers. My mother reared me to eat whatever was put in front of me, and so I eat. Dabbing jelly from my beard with a paper napkin as thin as the pages of the Gideons' Bibles, I look around. At 6:30 this Saturday morning, every seat is occupied. Why are we all here? Why are we wolfing down this dull, this dangerous, this terrible grub?

It's not for lack of alternatives. Bloomington is ringed by the usual necklace of fast-food shops. Or you could walk from Ladyman's to restaurants that serve breakfast in half a dozen languages. Just five doors away, at the Uptown Cafe, you could dine on croissants and espresso and quiche.

So why are we here in these swaybacked booths eating poorly cooked food that is bad for us? The answer, I suspect, would help to explain why so many of us are so much bigger than we ought to be. I sniff, and the aroma of lard and peppery sausage, frying eggs and boiling coffee, jerks me back into the kitchen of my grandparents' farm. I see my grandmother, barefoot and bulky, mixing biscuit dough with her blunt fingers. Then I realize that everything Ladyman's serves, she would have served. This is farm food, loaded with enough sugar and fat to power a body through a slogging day of work, food you could fix out of your own garden and chicken coop and smokehouse and pigpen, food prepared without spices or sauces, cooked the quickest way, as a woman with chores to do and a passel of mouths to feed would cook it. From the first clearings in the woods two centuries ago right down to the gigantic corn-and-soybean spreads of today, farming in these parts has never allowed time for dawdling in the kitchen.

"Hot up that coffee, hon?" the waitress asks.

"Please, ma'am," I say, as though answering my grandmother.

On those fishing trips, my father stopped at places like Ladyman's because there he could eat the vittles he knew from childhood, no-nonsense grub he never got at home from his wife, a city woman who had studied nutrition, and who had learned her cuisine from a Bostonian mother and a Middle Eastern father. I stop at places like Ladyman's because I am the grandson of farmers, the son of a farm boy. If I went from booth to booth, interviewing the customers, most likely I would find hay and hogs in each person's background, maybe one generation back, maybe two. My sophisticated friends would not eat here for love or money. They will eat peasant food only if it comes from other countries—hummus and pita, fried rice and prawns, liver pâté, tortellini, tortillas, tortes. Never black-eyed peas, never grits, never short ribs or hush puppies or shoofly pie. This is farm food, and we who sit here and shovel it down are bound to farming by memory or imagination.

With the seasoning of memory, the slithery eggs and gummy toast and rubbery jam taste better. I lick my platter clean.

Barely slowing down as she cruises past, the waitress refills my coffee once more, the oil-slicked brew jostling in the glass pot. "Need anything else, sugar?"

My nostalgic tongue wins out over my judgment, leading me to ask, "Could I get some biscuits and honey?"

"You sure can."

The biscuits arrive steaming hot. I pitch in. When I worked on farms as a boy, loading hay bales onto wagons and forking silage to cows, shoveling manure out of horse barns, digging postholes and pulling barbed wire, I could eat the pork chops and half a dozen eggs my neighbors fed me for breakfast, eat cornbread and sugar in a quart of milk for dessert at lunch, eat ham steaks and mashed potatoes and three kinds of pie for supper, eat a bowl of hand-cranked ice cream topped with maple syrup at bedtime, and stay skinny as a junkyard dog. Not so any longer. Not so for any of us. Eat like a farmer while living like an insurance salesman, an accountant, a beautician, or a truck driver, and you're going to get fat in a hurry. Where true farmers have always stored their food in root cellars and silos, in smoke shacks and on canning shelves, we carry our larders with us on haunches and ribs.

The Gideons file out, Bibles under their arms, bellies over their belts.

With the last of my biscuits I mop up the honey, thinking of the long path the wheat traveled from midwestern fields to my plate, thinking of the clover distilled into honey, of grass become butter, the patient industry of cows and bees and the keepers of cows and bees. Few of us still work on the land, even here in Indiana. Few of us raise big families, few of us look after herds of animals, few of us bend our backs all day, few of us build or plow or bake or churn. Officials of the Farm Bureau and Secretaries of Agriculture brag that only 4 percent of our population feeds the other 96 percent. If we honored that work more, instead of bragging we might regret that so few of us practice it, we might know how the food reaches our table, and we might also take better care of the earth.

I am stuffed. I rise, stretch, shuffle toward the cash register. The woman in the fringed vest looks up from her *Cosmopolitan* as I pass her booth. She might figure me for a carpenter, noticing my beard, the scraggly hair down over my collar, my banged-up hands, my patched jeans, my flannel shirt the color of the biscuits I just ate, my clodhopper boots. Or maybe she'll guess mechanic, maybe garbage man, electrician, janitor, maybe even farmer.

I pluck a toothpick from a box near the cash register and idly chew on it while the waitress makes change. "You hurry back," she calls after me.

"I will, ma'am," I tell her.

On the sidewalk out front of Ladyman's, I throw my toothpick in a green trash barrel that is stenciled with the motto, "Fight Dirty." I start the car, wincing at the sound of three cylinders clapping. I remember yesterday's rainwater shimmering in the basement, remember the house empty of my family, who are away frolicking with relatives. Before letting out the clutch, I let out my belt a notch, to accommodate those biscuits. Thirty-three inches. One inch closer to the ranks of the fat. I decide to split some wood this morning, turn the compost from the right-hand bin to the left, lay up stones along the edge of the wildflower bed, sweat hard enough to work up an appetite for lunch.

YARD BIRDS

GEESE HAVE HIT TOWN. NOT THE CANADA GEESE
that swoop down with raucous honks onto local ponds
in spring and fall, breaking their journeys to and from
the north country—no, these plump birds pose mutely
in yards, stolid concrete, the hint of a smile on their
beaks. Most of the beaks are painted orange and the bodies white, although here and there you will see brown
breasts and green necks simulating mallards, or the mus-
tard yellow of a dime store chick, or even the swirling
clownish colors of a wood duck. As often as not, a cap
or bonnet perches on the beaming head, and from the
scrawny neck dangles a bow tie or bib.

The plastic flamingos are still around, but their numbers have dwindled. No longer preening beside front

doors, as they used to when they were all the rage a couple of years ago, the flamingos have retreated to backyards, where they glow pinkly in the shadows of garages. The flamingos in turn had displaced the plywood cutouts of girls bending over to expose their polka-dot bloomers. And the exhibitionist girls had squeezed out the ducks with revolving wings, which had squeezed out the mirrored gold balls, which had squeezed out the meditative deer, which had squeezed out the black jockeys bearing lanterns, and so on back and back to the tusks and totems displayed by our shaggy ancestors before the mouths of caves.

It's a Darwinian struggle for space out there on the lawns. At the moment, as I say, the ascendant species hereabouts are geese. You can buy them painted or unpainted, dressed or bare, at feed stores, hardware stores, nurseries, roadside stands, and twenty-four-hour groceries.

The people who buy them tend to live in what the realtors call starter neighborhoods, where small frame houses mix with trailers and railroad sidings and evangelical churches. By contrast, in the ritzy neighborhoods (toward which, as toward heaven, the starters are presumably aiming), where swollen mansions squat on two-acre lots of poison-perfect grass, you will find nary a goose, nor a daisy pinwheel, nor any other vulgar ornament. The higher the rent, in other words, the fewer the lawn decorations.

My own neighborhood is, I suppose, midway on the ladder between humble start and glitzy finish, a sort of resting place for real estate climbers. The houses are mainly of two stories, old enough for termites but too young for historical plaques, sheathed in clapboard or limestone or brick, surrounded by huge trees and tiny yards. Within the compass of an after-dinner walk from our porch, you can find a menagerie of statuary—scarecrows, Kewpies, raccoons, gnomes, you name it. But instead of posing boldly, as they would on the far side of the tracks, the figurines in my neighborhood peep out from the cover of ferns, or hide in overgrown flower beds, or lean against the stems of birdbaths, secretive and shy. I suspect their owners feel toward them a mixture of shame and affection, roughly what my twelve-year-old son, Jesse, feels about his stuffed animals, which he keeps tucked away beneath the covers of his bed. Boys on the brink of teenhood are not supposed to sleep with teddy bears. Homeowners on the brink of prosperity are not supposed to relish the company of plaster dwarfs and plastic frogs.

Why is my own yard innocent of statues? Because we're aesthetes? Because we're snobs? I raised the question over blueberry pancakes one recent Saturday, by suggesting that our lawn could use a concrete goose or two. Long experience had taught my wife, Ruth, daughter Eva (now seventeen), and Jesse to ignore my cockamamie remarks unless I persisted. I persisted. "So what would you guys think about a pair of geese flanking the front steps?"

"Right," said Jesse with a snort.

"You think I'm kidding?"

"You've got to be kidding," said Eva.

"He's kidding," my wife assured them.

"I'm serious. I like those geese. You see them all over."

"You sure do," Jesse muttered.

"Wearing baseball caps and hula skirts and aprons," Eva observed. "Or dressed up like cowboys and pirates, with eye-patches and six-shooters. Sleaze city."

"I just want a couple of geese, that's all. No costumes. No painted smirks. No lipstick."

"Look, Dad," said Jesse, "if you have to junk up our yard, why don't you go all the way and put in mermaids and pigs and Mickey Mouse and dancing mushrooms?"

"Don't encourage him," said Ruth.

"Get really tacky," Eva suggested, "and go for the peasant in a sombrero leading a donkey. Or the black boy in a straw hat fishing from a bridge. Or the little boy and girl in the Dutch outfits, kissing."

"Is this one of those mid-life crisis deals?" Jesse asked while pouring syrup on a fresh stack of pancakes.

"Your father is kidding," Ruth insisted.

Eva sighed. "I can just see my friends coming up the walk between rows of flamingos decked out in tuxedos and tutus. 'This is my dad's idea of cute,' I'll say, and they'll say, 'Maximum weird.'"

"No flamingos," I said. "And no peasants or lantern boys. Just geese."

"But Dad," my son protested, his lips bruised from blueberries, "if you put plain old geese out there, people will think you *mean* it."

Shrewd as any twelve-year-old who sees through his father's bluff, Jesse forced me to admit that I could not put a goose or any other concrete species in our yard without also putting my tongue in my cheek. I would only be playing. But what of those troops of ornaments that decorate other lawns? Surely they are not all meant

as jokes. Surely some are meant as art. And a few, at
least, must be icons to household gods.

Certain yards are clearly designed to amuse us. For
example, just a few blocks from my place, over on East
Grimes, there's a bungalow with a lot half the size of a
tennis court featuring more than a hundred figures. A
leopard takes its ease in the shadow of Donald Duck.
Plywood tulips encircle plywood bears. A shark with jaws
agape breaches beside a skunk. Sad-eyed dogs loaf next
to happy-eyed leprechauns. The lion does indeed lie
down with the lamb. In this charmed space, the Darwinian struggle of lawn ornaments has given way to the
peaceable kingdom. It is as though refugees from a freak
show and the denizens of Saturday morning cartoons had
wandered into a zoo, and the entire motley crew had
been frozen in place by a sorcerer. To make sure we understand that the whole yard is enclosed in quotation
marks, the owners have raised in the midst of it a sign:
PLEASE DO NOT FEED THE ANIMALS.

Usually, however, there are no clear signs, no quotation marks telling us when to smile. If you put a bonnet on your goose, are you winking at us, saying it is all
a gag? Or do you think a goose looks better in a bonnet?
If you display a pair of chickens chatting on your limestone bench, or a trio of roly-poly pigs in bib overalls
gnawing ears of corn, are you smiling up your sleeve, or
are you recalling Grandpa's farm? If you border your walk
with mushrooms shaped like our local delicacy, the mo-
rel, but gigantic, their spongy heads the size of footballs,
do you mean for us to grin, or to lick our lips?

Pondering these ambiguities, I bicycle west of the
courthouse square to Fairview, stronghold of statues. It

is an appealing neighborhood, bounded on one side by Rosehill Cemetery, where fans of Hoagy Carmichael gather each year on the composer's birthday to pour whiskey over his grave; on the opposite side by a public housing project; on a third side by railroad cuts; and on the fourth by lumberyards and truck lots and a wasteland of scrap metal. The air crackles, not only on Sundays, with the fervor of evangelical churches: Apostolic Lighthouse, Pentecostal Faith Assembly, Mercy Mission ("You Tried Everything and Everything Has Failed—Try Jesus"). The streets hum with cottage industries, beauty shops and barbershops and car repair shops, perpetual yard sales, shingles offering to upholster furniture or haul trash. The cars in the neighborhood are older and bigger than elsewhere in town—bigger *because* they are older—with a higher percentage from Detroit, and a fair number propped on concrete blocks, their hoods yawning. Laundry flaps on lines. The men are partial to long sideburns, and the women favor beehive hairdos. A refreshing number of children play outdoors, air conditioning and cable television not having reached here in force. Old people live right next door to young couples, and grandparents supervise babies from porch swings.

Here also one finds yard ornaments in abundance, forthright and unapologetic. Take, for example, the two concrete Indians in feathered headdresses and war paint that sit on brick posts out front of Intricate Ink Tattoo Studio. Arms and legs crossed, the chiefs are solemn, and so is the manner of their display. I can only believe they are meant seriously, as seriously as the American flags that fly here more abundantly than anywhere else in town, as seriously as the spray-painted message on a

nearby railroad overpass, which warns: NO PILLS DOPE
KILLS. You are looking at art, the statues say. Admire us,
then come inside and get your tattoos.

Or consider the daisy pinwheels twirling in flower
beds, the plywood silhouettes of cardinals and bluejays
planted in side yards, the cacti and rabbits and alert deer
and, yes, even the pink flamingos. In this house we love
nature, such ornaments declare. So what if the same
images can be found on cheap greeting cards and shower
curtains? They are still fingers pointing toward the
wildness.

Other lawn decorations point to the past, invoking
farm and frontier. There are barrels, ox-yokes, anvils and
plows, pumps and windmills, dinner bells and wishing
wells, tractor tires painted white, and wagon wheels galore. There are statues of a pioneer couple, the husband
stalwart in fringed buckskin, the wife pious in a print
dress, a scarlet Bible clutched to her breast. Concrete
hogs and hens and cows speckle the lawns like totems
of the dinner table, as though to say, from these sacred
animals comes our meat.

Or, finally, before I leave the neighborhood, take
the apartment in the low-income housing project,
around whose front door cluster ten figures, including a
swan, a pelican, two chickens, three geese (one in bonnet, one in bowler hat and bow tie), another Indian
(this one standing), and a dog. The dog is modeled on
the attentive white pooch from the RCA record label,
ears pricked forward, listening to his master's voice. Instead of gazing into the horn of a victrola, however, this
dog gazes at the door of the apartment, as though waiting
for his master or mistress to appear. And when the own-

ers do appear—the man and woman, say, who have purchased and arranged these statues—what do they behold? I think they see exactly what the Medici beheld
when surveying a gallery of sculptures by Michelangelo
and Donatello. I think they see beauty. I think they see
tokens of the world's shapeliness. Like the Renaissance
dukes, the collectors of yard ornaments buy the art they
can understand and afford. And if the beauty they prize
is different from what the dukes or you or I might seek,
the craving is the same.

On the way home from Fairview, I pedal by the
White Rabbit gift emporium on Indiana Avenue. The
window is filled with inflated palm trees, fishing nets, a
mural of girls in bikinis, all as backdrop to a family of
flamingos. Not just any flamingos, the boxes proclaim,
these are "The Original Pink Flamingoes by Don Feath-
erstone," autograph edition. For ten dollars you can own
a pair. And you should own a pair, according to White
Rabbit, for a sign identifies these items as

COOL STUFF
YOU HAVE TO HAVE.

"Camp" and "kitsch" and "cool" all rhyme with "condescension." I keep on pedaling.

Our yard remains innocent of ornaments. Yet I still
have a hankering for geese. If I were to buy a pair, I know
where I would go—not to the grocery or hardware store,
but east on Route 46 to a trailer parked by the roadside
between the Nashville Alps ski slope (elevation 500
feet) and the Little Nashville Opry. A hand-lettered
square of cardboard offers them for fifteen dollars each.

I have met the old man who mixes and pours the concrete into molds, eighty-two pounds per bird, and the young woman who paints the geese with three coats of exterior latex.

"I want them to look beautiful for years," she tells me, "I want them to shine, I want them to glow."

The geese are her prize works, but she is almost as proud of the eagles, the cowboys and cowgirls, the Indians in full regalia, the cartoon characters and cupids and swans. They leave her lot in pickups, station wagons, hatchbacks, and go to populate the local yards. One day an archaeologist, excavating our town from beneath the sediment of ash and beer cans and fast-food wrappers, will be able to reconstruct something of our days and dreams by exhuming these lumps from our vanished lawns.

JAILHOUSE
BLUES

In JULY, WHEN THE WEATHER INLAND WAS FIT ONLY FOR lizards, I drove with my family to Cape Cod and spent a week loafing on that shifty hook of sand, chilling myself in the sea, sleeping nights in a shingled hut that used to be the Truro town jail. Neighbors still referred to our hut as The Jail, although it had long since been moved from the town into the woods, where it was enjoying a second career as yet another cottage for rent to ocean-hungry tourists. Coming from landlocked Indiana, we Sanders were about as hungry for ocean as any creatures without gills or webbed fingers could be.

We drove up to The Jail along parallel ruts in the sand, our muffler scraping anthills. Whitewashed inside and out, with the limbs of pitch pines and scrub oaks

brushing against the eaves and waist-high grasses flour-
ishing right up to the stoop, the cottage looked as
though it had sprouted there in the woods, like a gleaming cubical mushroom. Truro must not have suffered
much crime in the old days, to judge by the size of The
Jail. One sheriff, a deputy, and four inmates would have
filled the place. The original building was a two-story
box, with a single ground-floor room scarcely big enough
to swing the proverbial cat in, and a short-tailed cat at
that. Here, as I imagine it, the sheriff and deputy played
cards and kept glancing out the window, their eyes
peeled for trouble. The upstairs was divided into a pair
of cramped rooms with sloping ceilings, and here the
prisoners must have agreed to stay. They could hardly
have been *forced* to stay, for the casements around the
windows showed no evidence of steel bars, and the
flimsy doors and walls would have yielded to a casual fist.
A wing had been tacked onto one side of the box, to
accommodate a mossy bathroom and a galley kitchen,
the latter so narrow that you could burn your tail on the
stove while doing dishes in the sink. (I proved this by
experiment.) There was not a plumb wall, level floor, or
square joint in the whole rickety structure, which might
have been cobbled together over a drunken weekend by
a cross-eyed carpenter.

Our landlords had covered the largest gaps and holes
with flattened cans, to discourage mice. They encouraged spiders, however, and asked that we leave the cob-
webs in place, the better to snag mosquitoes and green-
head flies. There were quite evidently more flies and
mosquitoes than the webs could handle. These landlords, a hearty couple nearly as old as the century, were

longtime stalwarts of the Communist Party whose dis-
illusionment with America stretched back into the
1930s. Skeptical about private property, they took their
landlord status with several grains of irony. I had been
taught in childhood to expect cloven hoofs and forked
tails from communists, but could see no devilish defor-
mities in this genial pair. On the day of our arrival they
served us peppermint tea from cups of English bone
china, and told us stories of real jails where they and
their comrades had served time. (A curious phrase: to
serve time. As though time itself were the turnkey, as
though the proof of our liberty were the power to make
time serve *us*.) Between our landlords' tales and the
name of our cottage, even though I was footloose and
free on vacation I could not get the dreary business of
imprisonment out of my head.

This is merely one of my perversities, to brood on
lack in the midst of plenty, to think of aging flesh while
I bounce a baby in my arms, to imagine loneliness while
I am laced in talk with friends, and to remember jails all
during a week of utter freedom. It is a noxious trait,
which causes my wife and children to grit their teeth.
Knowing this, most of the time I keep my gloom under
a bushel. But there it flickers, all the same, a candle of
darkness.

IN THE MINIATURE BEDROOM I shared with my son Jesse
on the second floor of The Jail, the sloped ceiling kept
me from standing upright, and when the trundle bed was
pulled out, there was no floor left on which to stand at
all. As I lay there at night, listening to Jesse's guiltless

breath and to bobwhites wooing from nearby trees, I remembered sleeping in a refrigerator carton when I was a child. The cardboard box rested lengthwise in the mouth of the barn, end flaps left open for window and door, a bit of old carpet for mattress, a pillow and blanket for comfort, a flashlight for reassurance. Letting in sun and moon and stars, the box made a cozy nest for several nights. Then one morning I woke in utter blackness. I shoved against the end flaps, but they would not open. My last rational move was to switch on the flashlight, which promptly winked out when I used it to bang on the walls. Whereupon I went berserk. I became pure animal in a trap, kicking and yelling and flailing. I was an earthquake of fear. My ruckus kept me from hearing the amused grunts of the two neighbor boys who had stolen into the barn during the night and taped shut and barricaded my box. They had vamoosed by the time I battered my way out. I glared at my playhouse, which had become, with the closing of window and door, a prison. I emptied the box and stomped it flat and dragged it into the pasture and burned it. I did not stop shaking for an hour.

The mere recollection of that episode, as I lay upstairs in The Jail, with Jesse's breath and quail song filling the tiny room, was enough to keep sleep at bay. I remembered stories of kids who rubbed their parents the wrong way and got chained up in attics or basements, to age there and die like tethered dogs. I debated where I would rather be trapped—in an attic, which would be hot in summer, cold in winter, but dry at least, or in a basement, which would keep an even temperature the year round, but would also be damp and dark and snaky.

The very names for jail musicked through my head. Hoosegow, calaboose, slammer, stir, poky, cooler, jug, and clink. I remembered hearing about a slumlord in Los Angeles who, convicted of neglecting his properties, was sentenced to live for a month in one of his own tumbledown, rat-infested, cockroachy tenements. He was fitted with a beeper that would radio the police if he strayed more than fifty yards from the building. How would it feel, I wondered, to be caught in a web of electronics? I wondered also about those who imprison themselves. I thought of hermits, shut up in their unlit cells. I thought of Houdini, that virtuoso of confinement, who no sooner escaped than he was begging to be manacled again, wrapped in straitjackets, locked in cages, buried alive. In short, my candle of darkness burned with a long wick.

When I did finally drift off to sleep, afloat on my trundle bed, there was an edge of panic to my dreams. That first night I dreamed of a black bear slouching through the white cedar swamps of Cape Cod. My bear crawled into caves and hollow logs, where it stuck fast, or fell into pits, or tripped snares and went hurtling pawsfirst into the air, or bumbled into cleverly disguised cages. There was no disguise to the dream. In the morning, reflecting on this nightmare of entrapment, I was disappointed with my uninventive psyche.

THE NEXT DAY, friends guided us along an obscure path to the ocean, a path so obscure in fact that we were not surprised, on looking down from the outermost dune, to see only four other souls on the beach. The tang of salt raised the hairs on my neck, as if out of the blue the scent of a beast had challenged me. I howled. Dizzied by air and ocean, I was halfway down the dune before I realized that the four souls, each one basking on a towel or blanket, were stark naked. Disturbed by our noisy arrival, like herons roused from their brooding grounds, the sunbathers rose with gestures of indignation, pulled on their togs, and scuffed away over the sand.

Now as it happens, deep woods and mountaintops and ocean beaches always make me itch to fling off my clothes. Nature in the raw calls to nature in the raw. I usually keep this impulse—and myself—under wraps. But the itch is there. So I was sorry to have scared away these innocuous nudists. It is illegal to go naked on the Cape Cod National Seashore—just one more instance of the government's concern for our welfare—although I gather that park rangers, after gazing through binoculars to make sure of what they are seeing, warn offenders without arresting them.

Not all authorities are so indulgent. Near where I live in southern Indiana, a young woman was recently hauled into court for sunning in her backyard while wearing only the lower half of a bikini. One of her neighbors, offended by the spectacle, had called the police, who responded with even more than their usual zeal. Complaining that men had turned breasts into sexual baubles, the woman insisted upon her right to dress as she pleased in her own yard. For a month, the subject of bosoms enlivened the letters column in the local newspaper.

I thought of that embattled sunbather while these Cape Cod nudists trudged away, and I wondered if she would be locked up for having unfettered her own flesh. The case is pending. The two-year-old who lives next door to us back home in Indiana goes naked most of the summer, like a wood sprite. I see her flitting across the lawn, at perfect ease in her body, and I know there will come a day when the force of self-consciousness, if not of law, will squeeze her into clothes.

On other days, on other Cape Cod beaches, we saw acres of male and female flesh, lawfully clad in swimsuits. Many of the suits—mere scraps of cloth held in place by elastic bands—left little to the imagination. This did not prevent my imagination from working, however. I remembered how the mothers I knew as a boy would speak of certain loud and brassy girls as jailbait. A skirt worn too high above the knee, a blouse unbuttoned too far below the throat, a sultry way of laughing from the belly or of toying with shoulder-length hair was enough to identify the species. What would those mothers make of this beach teeming with nearly naked loungers? Before I was old enough to feel the full gravity of girls, I puzzled over how such bait could land a boy in jail. Were males mere fish to nibble at female hooks? There came a day, of course, when my blood put an end to my puzzling, and then I would glance furtively at the dangerous hussies, fearful that a direct stare would hurl me headlong behind bars.

I had a few half-baked notions about jails. My father's father had been a prison warden in Mississippi for a spell, and he told me dark tales of that place. The inmates wore dingy overalls striped with black, as heavy as canvas, and they left their cells only to exercise and to break stone for highways. Every man's name was entered in a logbook, and if he died before parole his name would be crossed through with an inky line. Riding by penitentiaries in the family car, I often saw the arms of prisoners thrust from windows, languid pale arms waving like the tentacles of undersea creatures.

Along about the time I began to feel the fierce bodily tug of girls, our school took a field trip to the county jail. I suppose the visit was meant to scare us into becoming upright citizens. It scared me, if not into uprightness, then at least into lifelong wariness about the law. The jail was a gray cement hulk, housing gray steel cells, filled with gray drooping men and women and boys. Boys not much older than my classmates and I, with homely backwoods faces like ours. The place reeked of urine and sweat—barn smells I knew and did not mind—but it reeked also with a smell new to me, a stench I came to identify as compounded of boredom, humiliation, and hopelessness: the stench of captivity.

DURING OUR WEEK on the Cape I generally avoided the news, figuring the world at the end of our vacation would still be in pretty much the same sticky mess. But one morning I picked up a *Boston Globe* to find out how the dismal Red Sox were doing. They were doing dismally. I should have quit after reading the box score. Instead, I browsed through the rest of the paper. There I sat out front of The Jail, loafing and taking my ease on a lawn chair in the sunshine, considering myself immune to the world's ills, when my lazy eye fell on an article about the population crunch in American prisons. I read it through and felt predictably bad. A few numbers stuck in my head like cockleburs: over the past fifteen years, our inmate population has tripled, amounting now to 600,000; in the United States, one out of every thirty-five men is either in jail or skulking about under the suspicious eyes of parole officers; American blacks are imprisoned at a rate higher than for any other group anywhere else in the world, including South Africa; and during the week of our vacation about one thousand more of our fellow citizens would be locked up. The stench of captivity rose in my nostrils.

Since my gloom threatened to obscure the family sunlight, I folded the paper away and suggested that we all go blueberrying. We drove the back roads, scanning the woods, and eventually found a good patch of bushes along the rusty iron fence of a cemetery. Long before my plastic bowl was filled, I quit picking berries and went strolling among the lichen-spangled tombstones, on the lookout for queer inscriptions. Aside from the three Sanders who were picking and the one who was snooping, the only other visitor was a man who sat in his car near the center of the graveyard, his tattooed arm crooked out the window and his radio blaring. What on earth was he listening to? At first I could make out nothing except a mumble of talk. Then as I drew near the car, I recognized the voice of a retired admiral, who was testifying before Congress about his role in the conduct of a secret war, which he and some cronies both inside and outside the government had been carrying on in various bleeding corners of the world. There was in the admiral's voice the fudgy caution of a man who knows a slip of the tongue might put him in handcuffs. Before answering questions, he consulted his attorney in whispers that sounded over the radio like the filing of fingernails. This was more ugly news I would rather not have heard, not here and now, not during the tattered remains of a vacation.

Beyond the reach of radio, the dead beneath my feet did not stir. Having them for company reminded me of stories about poor souls who had been buried alive, souls who woke up in the grave and clawed their fingers to stubs and composed notes in blood on the inside of coffin lids before expiring. When it dawned on me as a child that the bodies shut up in caskets were shut up there for good, I lost my taste for sleeping in cardboard boxes. Indeed, I lost my taste for sleeping anywhere. To close my eyes on darkness was to bang down a lid, perhaps forever. Eventually, after months and months of terror-stricken nights, I persuaded myself that sleep is not burial, a bed is not a coffin, that return of daylight is guaranteed. It was and remains a shadowy belief, at which I dare not peer too closely, for fear of seeing right through it to a nothingness on the other side.

WE NIBBLED BLUEBERRIES on our way back from the graveyard, saving only enough for the next morning's pancakes. I awoke at five that next morning, our last on the Cape, and tiptoed outside to see what the world had to offer. A fox had been down our lane, leaving dimpled pawprints in the tawny sand. I followed the tracks as they meandered from lane to field of purple beach peas and saltspray roses, from field to woods of oak and pine, from woods to lane and back again to field and woods. There was no hurry in this trail. The fox must have been in a contemplative mood, as I was.

From a brushy hill, where cows once grazed and where tufts of rye still grew as a reminder of farms, I could see across half a mile of marsh to the bay. I walked to the shore through lavender light, past continents of reeds that waved their blond plumes higher than my head. Sand lapped over the buckled blacktop of the road. Poison ivy climbed the speed limit signs, and vines gripped the telephone poles. On dunes overlooking the beach, the outermost cottages perched on stilts, like flightless and gawky birds that would go smash in the first gale. In these reminders that we can make nothing permanent, there was a taste of freedom. Even those boxes we build for shelter and freely enter, even our clothes, even our jobs and reputations are jails of a sort. We need to escape them now and again, need to imagine them falling away from us like old skins, if we are to keep from smothering.

There was a taste of freedom also in the blueberry pancakes, a wild and tangy savor. We moved out of The Jail after breakfast and joined the Saturday morning crowd of those who had finished their holidays. Those who were just arriving thronged the opposite lane of the highway. Seeing the twin streams of cars, one flowing onto the Cape, one flowing off, I could not avoid thinking of other natural passages—the tides, the migration of alewives and seabirds, the arrival and retreat of sunlight. Doubtless this thought occurs to multitudes each year, as they are stuck in traffic jams on this skinny peninsula. A craving for escape drives us to these exposed places—to the margins of oceans and the tops of mountains—and then chains of duty drag us back home. We go and come as though caught in the inhalation and exhalation of a great breath, without knowing who or what it is that breathes.

LIVING

SOULS

THE AGENT AT THE PAN AM COUNTER IN INDIANAPOLIS
had to search a long while before he discovered the tomato-red luggage tag marked MOSCOW, USSR. The destination was not a common one for travelers from Indiana. For this particular traveler—an avid reader of
Russian literature since high school, a skeptical admirer
of Marx, a child of the Cold War—this was a first visit
to the Soviet Union. What I knew of that vast and various land had come entirely from television and newspapers and books. What I knew had been refracted
through the lenses of my own country, which, in official
policy and popular sentiment, had regarded the USSR
as a mortal enemy since before my birth.

The tomato-red tag was not affixed until an amiable guard had groped through my suitcase for bombs. "You're clean," he announced. I did not feel clean. I was running with sweat, less from anxiety than from the fierce August heat I had rushed through to arrive at this cautious place. Between here and that other cautious place a third of the way around the earth, my luggage would be searched repeatedly, my papers inspected, my body scanned, as I passed through layer after layer of misgiving.

The Pan Am agent, who was the last man wearing a wig I would see before my return to the United States, frowned at my visa, which rendered my name in Cyrillic as CKOT CAHDEPC. "I can't make heads or tails of that," he said, returning the document to me with a shrug. I could read the visa, as a result of having studied Russian over the summer, but what I could say in that musical language was less than the babble of a Soviet toddler.

A lusty babble of Russian lilted all around me on the flight from New York to Moscow, the voices of emigrés returning for family visits. "It is our first visit home," a fiftyish woman told me from across the aisle. "Before, we were afraid to return. But now it is a new day." This particular new day was in August of 1988.

My seatmates were two Marines, just old enough to buy Bloody Marys from the stewardess, one reading *Newsweek*, the other engrossed in *People*, both wearing earphones over their crew cuts. They were on their way for a tour of six months at the American Embassy in Moscow. Why so brief a stint? "They rotate us through there fast, to keep us from fraternizing," said one Marine.

Fraternizing: treating the enemy as though he were a brother. His use of the word brought to mind old photographs of rival soldiers at the front hugging one another during a cease-fire. An elderly woman whose purple tour badge identified her as Bertha paused in the aisle to tell the Marines, "I feel much safer, knowing you boys are going over there with us."

At midnight Indiana time I set my watch forward nine hours. I had lost a night. "Now it is a new day," the Russian woman had told me. How new the Soviet day in fact was, and what the human weather promised to be in Moscow, were questions I carried with me across the ocean.

BEYOND THE PASSPORT BOOTHS and customs gates and security fences in Moscow's Sheremetyevo International Airport, hundreds of eager faces waited to greet friends and relatives who had arrived on my flight. The man who waited for me was a stranger, husky as a mason in his gray pin-striped suit, with a brown flap of hair curling down over his forehead and quick eyes above a nervous half smile. Andrei Sergeyevitch Svetenco had reason to be nervous. He and his wife had learned only two days earlier that they would be hosting me during my week in Moscow. I could never discover exactly how they and their son had been selected from the city's nearly nine million people as a representative family. Aside from my name and nationality and profession, they knew nothing about me. To open their home and thoughts to an American writer, an outsider who would return to his own country and publish whatever he chose about their lives, was a brave and perhaps foolhardy act, about which Andrei, as he shook my hand in the lobby, must have been having second thoughts.

Andrei had been led to believe that I spoke Russian, but after our exchange of hellos he knew better. "You must forgive my poor English," he told me in good English, with a robust accent, rich in r's, that gave the words a pleasing weight in the ear. "I have no chance to practice speaking it."

"I understand you perfectly," I told him.

"But wait until I have something difficult to say!"

And so began our week-long dialogue, across two languages and two continents and two ways of life, a dialogue that would stretch Andrei's English and my understanding beyond the limits each of us had imagined.

Outside, the air was cooler by a season than the blistering air I had left in Indiana, more like October than August, and the light on this cloudless day was milder than the insistent corn-ripening sunlight of the Midwest. This gentle northern light shone on buildings and cars and clothes that were the shades of earth, charcoal and gray, buff and cream, making the world appear muted. Along the highway from the airport to the city there were no billboards to disrupt the somber tones, no garish franchises, no neon lights, few traffic signs. Instead there were trees, dark shaggy conifers and white birches that crowded up nearly to the pavement, giving one the sense that the forest was primary, the road secondary. Since childhood, when I had dreamed of making birchbark canoes worthy of Indians, I had loved these white trees with their inky slashes. In Moscow I was to see them everywhere I turned, in parks and playgrounds, on any patch of dirt large enough to support life, ghostly presences, glimmering.

On the drive from the airport, the first landmark Andrei pointed out to me was a monument of crossed black steel girders, an enlargement of the tank barricades from World War II, honoring the spot a few kilometers outside of Moscow where the Nazis were stopped in December 1941. The Soviet name for the prolonged bloodbath, in which some twenty million of her people died, is the Great Patriotic War. I was to see memorials to war and revolution and suffering planted in Moscow almost as thickly as the birches. As we sped past, two newlyweds were posing for photographs at the monument, the bride's white gown like a froth of bubbles against the black steel, the groom as dark as a raven, their smiles uncannily bright against the gloom of memory.

It is a custom in the Soviet Union for newlyweds to visit memorials to those who died in defense of the motherland. On his own wedding day twelve years earlier, Andrei had taken his new bride to lay flowers on the Tomb of the Unknown Soldier, in the shadow of the Kremlin wall. The wall with its towered gates flashed by our car as he told me this. The bride's name was Marina Nikolayova Filatova, a name she kept intact through marriage. "In our country it is rare for a woman to keep her family name," Andrei said. "But I wanted very much to marry her, so I did not object."

As we approached his apartment block, which is south of the meandering Moscow River, midway between the second and third ramparts of the ancient city, Andrei began to apologize. The building, like much of the city, like the entire society, was undergoing *peres-*

troika, reconstruction. Forgive the mess. I was used to mess, I told him, for my family and I had been renovating our old house piecemeal for a dozen years.

"You do the work yourselves?" he asked with surprise.

"Everything except the plumbing."

"Then maybe you can help us with our electricity!" He laughed. Already I could hear that Andrei had a gift for laughter, as others have a gift for storytelling or song.

Instead of a lawn, a thicket of saplings and bushes and weeds surrounded the apartment block. Everywhere in Moscow I was to find the apartments encircled by these young forests that looked at once unkempt and appealingly wild. We picked our way past fervent blue chicory and black-eyed Susans and Queen Anne's lace, a constellation of late summer blossoms familiar to me from Indiana, then past heaps of lumber and shattered bricks, past the vigilant eyes of old women on benches, *babushkas* wearing *babushkas,* some of them doubtless widows since the Great Patriotic War, past three locks, and so into a sunny corner flat on the seventh floor.

The woman who had defied convention by keeping her maiden name greeted us at the door. Marina Filatova seemed to possess, as the hollow bones of birds possess, the contradictory qualities of delicacy and strength. A slender woman with a valentine face given to pensive pouts and blazing smiles, elegant in movement, precise in speech, hair in dark brown curls to her shoulders and in bangs over dark shining eyes, she wore a white dress imprinted with red flowers. She was thirty-one at the time of my visit, a year younger than Andrei and eleven years younger than myself. During that week she would seem by turns girlish in her idealism and grandmotherly in her wisdom, as Andrei would seem by turns brash and sage. Although Marina pronounced the occasional English word with remarkable clarity, and she understood most of what I said to her, for the present she spoke only in Russian to Andrei, who translated her words into English for me. The language barrier, combined no doubt with her uncertainty about this Yankee guest, gave her the appearance of being shy.

Over dinner they began to sketch for me the outlines of their lives. Andrei is a historian, in charge of the cataloguing department in the Central State Archives for Historical Acts. Marina, a teacher at the Oil and Gas Institute, was on leave from her job while preparing to defend a graduate thesis.

"So you're a geologist?" I asked.

My question provoked laughter, followed by an awkward silence. I looked down at my plate, an array of sliced tomatoes, cucumbers, peppers, green peas, black and white bread, with a cheese-topped cutlet at the center, a delight for both eye and tongue, as every one of Marina's dishes would be.

"To tell you the truth," Andrei said at last, "what Marina teaches is the science of communism."

I took this to mean that she kept the young geologists at the Oil and Gas Institute on the straight-and-narrow, that Marina was, in effect, an ideological watchdog for the Party. As with so many other first judgments, this would later come to seem inane, a cartoonish oversimplification.

The dissertation she was preparing to defend explores the problem of contradictions in Soviet society.

Contradictions—as between the citizens and the bureaucracy, or between the workers and the state—were a "problem" because, according to Marx and Lenin, they should have disappeared with the coming of socialism. And yet there the contradictions were, as anyone with eyes could see. Was this an exciting time to study the question, because of *glasnost*, the new openness to debate? Yes, Marina replied, but it was also a time of uncertainty. Who would her examiners be, and how far would they permit her to go?

While Marina explained these matters through Andrei, I sipped my champagne, which, in keeping with Mr. Gorbachev's crusade against drunkenness, was non-alcoholic. "As in your own Prohibition," said Andrei, "some people begin making liquor at home. But even that is difficult, because sugar is rationed." I taught them the meaning of *bootlegger* and *moonshine* and *hooch*.

Their only child, an eight-year-old son named Mikhail, was spending the summer as usual with Marina's father and mother at the parents' dacha outside of Moscow. I would meet him on Tuesday. They invariably referred to the boy by his diminutive, Misha, which also happens to be the name for a bear cub, a folk mascot whose place in Soviet culture is akin to that of Mickey Mouse in the United States. In the afternoon, Marina excused herself to go pay Misha a visit.

Andrei and I took a long garrulous walk, down the avenues crowded with Saturday strollers, in and out of neighborhood shops, through the dappled shade of birches and maples in a section of Gorky Park called "The Garden of Un-boredom." To this American eye, accustomed to public eccentricity, the strollers appeared mannerly, restrained, the girls and women linked at the elbows, the boys clasping the hands of grandparents, faces composed, voices playing quietly on private channels.

To any American eye, the shops would have seemed meagerly stocked and drably decorated. On the other hand, because the Soviet economy does not run on the fuel of endless consumption, one is not constantly exhorted there, as one is in the United States, to buy, buy, buy! The sole item universally promoted in the streets and squares and media is the Soviet state, its heroic past and glorious future. One sees this in the slogans that are spelled out in electric letters along the rooflines of buildings, in signs on the hoardings of construction sites, in murals and posters and plaques, in documentaries and newscasts, in war memorials and grandiose statues. The intersection of Lenin Prospect and Kosygin Avenue, near Andrei and Marina's flat, is presided over by a gigantic statue of Cosmonaut Gagarin, the first human to orbit the earth, who is represented not as the compact intelligent man he actually was, but as a chromium superhero with bulging muscles. Whenever I felt oppressed by this constant promotion of the state, the system, the motherland, I recalled that in an American city there would have been even more urgent, ubiquitous pitches for cigarettes and motorcycles and beer. If the Soviets have made a religion of collective achievement, we have made a religion of private gratification.

My legs were rubbery from jet lag, my head woozy from new impressions. As we walked, Andrei chain-smoked Bulgarian cigarettes ("the taste of cabbage") and commented exuberantly on everything we passed. He perceived the city in four dimensions, three of space and one of time, for behind every building and street name and statue there was a history, which he recounted in fervent detail. Much of the visible past still reflected the rule of Joseph Stalin, whose name Andrei would introduce into our conversation dozens of times that week, always with loathing. According to that quintessential American, Henry Ford, "History is bunk." All of Moscow delivers a contrary message, for which my spirited companion was the ideal interpreter: the message that history is inescapable. History is in our bones. To ignore the past is to live as a fool.

Near midnight, after Marina's return from visiting Misha, the three of us took another walk, this time along the river to the enormous gothic tower of Moscow State University. Marina had studied philosophy and the science of communism in that tower, one of six colossal buildings ordered by Stalin to show that Moscow, like New York, was capable of skyscrapers. From the esplanade in front of the university, in the moon-shadow of a tall curving slide used for winter ski jumping, we gazed across the river at Moscow's web of lights. In the darkness it could have been any great city, half-asleep, half-awake, giving off the ferment of change.

"It is because Marina and I wish to be part of that change, to be in touch with what is happening in our society," said Andrei, "that we joined the Communist Party."

Thus he answered a question I had not asked.

"These days are like the time after the Revolution," said Marina, "when Lenin welcomed debate, disagreement, fresh ideas."

"Under Stalin, disagreement became a crime," said Andrei. "In the old days, a man thought one thing, dreamed another thing, and spoke something else. Now, we think and dream and say the same thing. What we used to whisper only in our kitchens, we now say on television, in the meeting halls, in the streets."

I WOKE ON SUNDAY to the grit of truck tires on Kosygin Avenue. Most of those trucks were olive drab army vehicles, as were most of the bulldozers, earthmovers, shovel loaders, and other heavy equipment I saw in Moscow. This gave to the streets the look of a city under martial law. And yet nearly all the drivers were civilians; the trucks hauled not weapons but cement and bread and steel. Eventually I realized that Soviet army vehicles, whose numbers mount so ominously in the reports delivered by the Pentagon to Congress, take the place of our own municipal fleets, utility company vans, private construction equipment, delivery trucks, and long-distance rigs. Instead of rusting on gravel lots, military equipment is put to use in the constant low-grade war to build and repair the city.

Still, I found the olive drab tone of the streets disquieting. During a childhood spent mostly in an arsenal, surrounded by soldiers and the machinery of war, I developed an allergy to militarism. Since the framers of our constitution warned against the danger of standing armies, a suspicion of soldiers has run deep in the American grain, perhaps never deeper than in those of us who came of age during the Vietnam War. In Moscow I encountered a people who view soldiers as heroes, builders, protectors, saviors. This attitude of respect, bordering on reverence, was evident in casual remarks, in museums and on television, in the jackets worn by older men decorated with ribbons and medals from the Great Patriotic War, in cemeteries where the tombs of commanders were heaped with flowers, in the memorials that served almost as shrines.

However useful it no doubt has been to the pursuit of the communist dream, the celebration of the military is not an invention of the Soviet era, but rather a persistent theme in Russian history. Most of the hospitals and churches in Moscow that have survived from czarist times were built to commemorate a victory—over the French, the Swedes, the Turks, the Finns, the Germans. The list of foes is a long one. For a millennium, the nation centered around Moscow has been invaded from every point of the compass, and has in turn expanded the area of its control in every direction. Over the course of the week, Andrei would speak not only of the struggle against Hitler, but of that against Napoléon in the nineteenth century, the Poles in the seventeenth, the Tatars in the sixteenth, the Mongols in the fourteenth. For him, as for his people, invasion is a present horror kept fresh by the waters of recollection.

On a Sunday morning television show about the Red Army, we saw volunteers cleaning up the radioactive debris from the crippled nuclear reactor at Chernobyl; we heard amputees recalling the war in Afghanistan. As of that week, half the Soviet troops had come home from the war, after thirteen thousand of their comrades had died and thirty-five thousand had been wounded, and the remaining troops were scheduled to return home within the next few months. Andrei reported these numbers with a sigh. When I suggested that his country had made the same mistake in Afghanistan that my country had made in Vietnam, he disagreed firmly, insisting that the Soviet Union had taken sides with the democratic forces, while the United States had backed the reactionaries.

Sunday was to be the most military of my days, as we followed the television show with a walk through Red Square and the Kremlin. "Our history begins here," said Andrei, thumping his shoe on the stones of the square, whose name originally meant not red but beautiful. This place of executions, revolutions, proclamations, and parades recalled for me newscast footage of troops marching and tanks wheeling in formation, missiles drawn on wagons past the faces of enraptured crowds, wizened rulers gazing down from the roof of Lenin's mausoleum. Andrei pointed out to me with satisfaction the place in the Kremlin wall to which Stalin, once displayed alongside Lenin in the mausoleum, had been demoted. One of the Politburo members who had voted for the demotion was Mikhail Gorbachev, himself now the central figure presiding over parades, a vigorous rather than a wizened man. Yet the parades these days are no less martial than before.

The Kremlin itself is a fortress, roughly triangular in shape, surrounded by a high crenelated wall. The river still flows along one flank, and in earlier times the other two were protected by a moat. Beyond the moat there were two circular ramparts, which are still visible on the map of Moscow as the paths of ring roads. The word *kremlin* itself originally meant a fortified stronghold. In-

side, the czars built palaces to hold their wealth, barracks
for troops, an arsenal for weapons, and cathedrals to capture God. Authority continues to emanate from this
place that was built to repel assaults. Entering through
one of the twenty towers, Andrei and I shuffled from
palace to cathedral to garden in the company of orderly
crowds. The only raised voices I heard were American.
The only visitors who wandered outside the zebra-striped
footpaths, provoking curt whistles and a wave of batons
from policemen, were American. I was embarrassed by
my own people, as I often am when abroad, and yet I
was also growing impatient with Soviet decorum. Where
was the play, the zest, the idiosyncracy in their lives?

As we retraced our steps through Red Square, Andrei remarked on a painter who slouched against a window sill as she worked. Until recently, he said, you
would not have seen such unruly behavior, people leaning on buildings! He also mentioned that he had been
puzzled to see American young people sitting on the floor
of the airport, even lying on the floor, instead of using
the chairs. The few times we saw a pedestrian jaywalk,
usually across a street that was empty of traffic, Andrei
never failed to shake his head at this lawless behavior.
I wondered what he would think of the students at my
university, the pedestrians in my town, or the children
in my home. Would they seem to him slovenly and way-
ward, or enviably uninhibited?

Although well-mannered themselves, Andrei and
Marina viewed this passion for public decorum with a
redeeming humor. When we met a skateboarder, one of
three I would see in Moscow, Andrei observed that older
people strongly disapproved of these reckless contrap-

tions, as they disapproved of break dancing. "But me, I would ride one, if my bones were younger!" It was another sign of the new leniency that police no longer broke up skateboarding tournaments nor chased dancers from the sidewalks. How far this public playfulness would be allowed to go, he could not say. On the Metro one night, Marina laughed at a wall placard, which listed fifty-two rules. "Fifty of them say what you may not do, and only two say what is allowed!" Despite their good humor, I took care not to stand out from the crowd. In walking, in speaking, in handling a fork, in everything I did all week, I was conscious of acting with restraint.

Marina's sense of propriety led us to move on Sunday evening from her and Andrei's flat, where the hot water was mysteriously out, to her parents' flat, which was vacant for the summer. A guest from America must be able to wash. I told her that cold water would do just fine. No, she insisted. Her parents had a couch that opened into a bed, a color television, hot water. We all would be more comfortable there. So we left the four worn but meticulously kept rooms, with their parquet floors and papered walls, their glass cases filled with books and china and Misha's war toys, and moved into three larger, better furnished rooms in northwestern Moscow, high in another apartment tower, higher than the derricks that bristled on the Moscow skyline. Here the carpets were plusher, the wallpaper fresher, the stove and refrigerator newer. The glass cases here contained even more books: poetry and novels, science fiction, mysteries, handsome collected editions of works by the great Russian and Soviet writers, along with volumes by cherished foreigners, such as Mark Twain and Jack London. There was indeed a color television in the living room as well as a black-and-white set in the kitchen, and the couch made a comfortable bed. But on Sunday night, at least, there was no hot water. It did not soothe Marina to learn that large sections of Moscow were temporarily without hot water. She was fit to be tied. She promised that in the morning she would heat water herself, on the stove. For tonight I must forgive her, forgive the city, forgive socialism.

WHENEVER SHE WORKED in the kitchen, Marina hummed along to music on the radio or to melodies playing in memory. While frying sausages for Monday's breakfast and heating water for our baths, she was humming a tune from *Jesus Christ, Superstar.* She and Andrei had come to like western music through listening to cassettes of the Beatles, Rolling Stones, Pink Floyd, and Deep Purple. Now they listened eagerly to such new Soviet groups as Bravo, Aquarium, Kino, Secret, and Nautilus Pompilus, which sing about social problems in the mournful rhythm of ballads or the raucous beat of rock. "It is music not only about teenage love," Andrei explained, "but about community, about grown people making a world together." For the same reason they cherished the music of their "bards," singers who speak of crime, prisons, injustice, war, the dark side of the socialist utopia. "Like your own Pete Seeger," said Andrei. "When I was a boy, all the time I listened to British and American pop music. Now, I prefer the bards and classics. Rachmaninoff, Mozart, Grieg!" Before the week was out, I heard works by all three composers on radios in taxis. One cabbie, who lowered the volume when the news came on, raised it again when he caught the opening measures of Rachmaninoff's second piano concerto. In cars and kitchens, the radio was always on, playing folk music from the more than a hundred ethnic groups of the Soviet Union and from around the world, playing symphonies and arias, big band combos and jazz. Among the few types of music I did not hear in Moscow were country-western and Muzak, both of which I was glad to do without.

The radio at one side of the kitchen table was tuned for my benefit to the English-language version of Radio Moscow, while on the opposite side the television murmured. We ate most of our meals in this cross fire of images and words. As on other days, our conversation over Monday's breakfast lasted two hours, beginning with shaved and sugared carrots at ten and ending with chocolates and coffee at noon. As he grew excited about politics or chess or sports, Andrei would get up and pace, every now and again consulting the tiny Russian-English dictionary he carried in his pocket. More composed, Marina would linger at the table or work at the sink. (She refused to let me clear my dishes, let alone wash them, as I would have done at home.) Lips pursed, she listened to Andrei's English, breaking in with her lilting Russian to correct or embroider on what he said.

"We need to recover a sense of pride," he declared that morning as he paced. "A sense of having power over our lives. Men do not exploit men here. We have overcome that problem. But we need to recover the spiritual dimension."

What about Marx's claim that consciousness and the realm of spirit were simply reflections of material conditions?

"The two are connected," said Marina, "but our material life will improve only when people feel they are masters of their lives. We must give control back to workers and farmers. We must have real democracy."

In recent months, encouraged by the example of Raisa Gorbachev, who teaches methods of social inquiry, Marina had interviewed men and women in factories. "They boiled over with emotions. They spoke of their fears, their frustrations, their hopes. For too long they have been silent. For too long no one has asked them what they truly want. I am convinced that we must change not only what they can buy in the stores, but what they feel in their hearts."

This was a constant theme in our talk, the need for a renewal of spirit, soul, heart alongside the economic transformation of Soviet society. In this era of *glasnost* and *perestroika,* when long-suppressed novels and films were appearing, when the media were criticizing the system, when the streets were buzzing with debate, Andrei and Marina sensed all around them the beginnings of a spiritual recovery.

The signs of change were plentiful. Construction of yet another war memorial in Moscow had recently been halted by public outcry against the design. Oil drilling in the Arctic had been halted by protests from native peoples concerned about pollution. The often fierce debates from the summer Party Congress had been reprinted verbatim in *Pravda* and broadcast on television, inspiring crowds to gather in Pushkin Park and carry on the debate in open air. The aftermath of the Chernobyl disaster, the explosion of a weapons train, the wreck of the Leningrad-Moscow express with much loss of life, the failure of a space rendezvous, all were frankly discussed on television during my stay, whereas even a year earlier such mishaps would have been concealed in bureaucratic silence. From the Republic of Georgia, where Andrei had once angered a roomful of men by refusing to drink a toast to Stalin, came the broadcast of a puppet show that bitterly and hilariously satirized the Stalinist regime. On Marina's bedside table, the current issue of *Novy Mir*, the journal of the writers' union, lay open to the first installment of *Dr. Zhivago*, the novel which had forced Pasternak into exile a generation earlier. In the same magazine a few months later would appear *1984*, long held to be an attack on communism.

Another token of the spiritual and cultural renaissance was the screening of films by Andrei Tarkovsky, who had been driven out of the Soviet Union during the Brezhnev era. "We call it the era of stagnation," said Andrei. At a cinema on Monday evening amid a hushed audience we watched Tarkovsky's *Sacrifice*. The original Swedish dialogue was translated by a phlegmatic Russian narrator, making the film incomprehensible to me in two languages. Andrei, too moved to speak during the movie, told me afterwards that it was about a man who cuts himself off from his son, his wife, his home, his work, in fulfillment of a vow he had made when praying that the world be spared a nuclear holocaust. Even in exile, the Soviet artist was brooding on war. When I asked Andrei to translate the line of text that appeared at the end of the film, he gestured that I must wait, and I saw that he was weeping. The last figure on screen was a boy who reminded Andrei and Marina of their own son, Misha. The closing text was a message of love addressed to Tarkovsky's son, back in the Soviet Union, whom Tarkovsky would never be allowed to see. "He died in exile, in 1986, the year he made the film," said Andrei. "That is wrong. That is deeply wrong. He was one of our geniuses. He should have been here in his own country, teaching us. Now, at least, we can see his work."

WHILE I SAVORED my dish of cheesecake soaked in gooseberry sauce on Tuesday morning, Andrei rubbed his eyes and complained about having to rise at such a beastly hour. Seven-thirty! From the bedroom came the sound of Marina singing. "She is a skylark, who likes to go to sleep early and get up early. But me, I am an owl. I prefer to stay up late and sleep even later." Misha was taking after him, becoming an owlet.

We had risen at this hour in order to go visit Misha in the country at his grandparents' dacha. In a hired car we drove the sixty kilometers west of Moscow. Andrei and Marina had no car of their own, nor would they be able to afford one for another twenty or thirty years, Andrei predicted with a laugh. They asked gingerly if I owned a car. Yes, I told them. And a house? Yes. Did my children have their own rooms? Yes, yes. Were the rooms full of toys? Was my house full of electronic gadgets? Were my closets full of clothes? Too full for my taste and my conscience, I answered. Did all Americans own so much? Not all, but many, perhaps too many for the good of the earth.

It must have seemed easy for one who owned so much to speak with misgiving about ownership. All week they hinted at a deeper question, without ever quite asking: Did I find their way of life humble by comparison to life in America? Did I find them poor? Had they asked, my answer would have exhausted our shared vocabulary. I would have told them I do not measure the quality of a life by the quantity of possessions. I would have said they live more elegantly, considerately, responsibly with their few things than do many Americans of my acquaintance who own far more. I would have said, quoting Thoreau, that a man is rich in proportion to the number of things he can do without. I would have said that their government, like mine, has lavished far too much wealth on weapons and soldiers, too little on daily needs, too much on public display and too little on private delight. No people in such an abundant land should have to wait in line for bread. No children in such an ingenious land should have to make do with shoddy toys. No archivist, no teacher, should have to spend a month's pay for a suit of clothes. Yes, their lives are harder than the lives of all but the poor in my country, and I do not sentimentalize hardship. I would like to see their stores full of useful and handsome and healthful goods. But I would also like to see our own stores full of such goods. I would not wish on my Soviet friends the acres of plastic, the billboards, the commercials, the highway sleaze, the mass delusion of fashion,

the endless borrowing against the future, and the pro-
digious waste that accompany prosperity in America.

At the village of Aprelyevka we turned from the
highway onto a side road that consisted of parallel concrete strips, broken at the joints and half-buried in mud
churned up by cows. The cows belonged to a collective
farm, across whose pastures the road had been roughly
laid. A few morose brown eyes gazed at us from the herd
as we lurched by. We also drew stares from a trio of mushroom gatherers clutching lumpy sacks and from an elderly couple who were hauling firewood on the chassis
of a baby buggy. Eventually we came to a cluster of about
one hundred cottages, encircled by a fence and set off
strikingly against the forest of birch and fir. Like all land
in the Soviet Union, this belongs to the State, which
loaned these few acres to veterans of the Great Patriotic
War for the creation of a gardening cooperative. It was
evident the cottagers took the word "gardening" seriously, for the lots of six hundred square meters had been
planted from boundary to boundary with vegetables and
fruit trees and flowers. Green and blossoming waves
lapped against the foundations, climbed the walls of
brick and board, flung tendrils above the fretwork of the
eaves onto the peaked metal roofs.

The walkway to Marina's parents' cottage was bor-
dered by red zinnias the size of my palm, scarlet salvia,
spiky asters, and nodding sunflowers higher than my
head. The cottage itself looked as though it might have
sprouted there, for it was made of knotty pine, varnished
inside and out so that it gleamed in the sunlight. Our
reception was loud and loving, first from Marina's father,

Nikolai Ivanovich Filatov, a retired army officer, genial and hearty, with a farmer's tan and a fringe of unruly gray hair; next from Marina's mother, Nina Petrovna Filatova, a retired nurse, gentle and beaming and happily flustered by the arrival of this American; then from Marina's sister, Lena, a large and tranquil woman of thirty-nine, on maternity leave from her job as an engineer; and then in shy succession by a trio of grandchildren, eight-year-old Misha and six-year-old Anya and eighteen-month-old Ivan, the latter pair belonging to Lena, all three as blond as cornsilk and as fresh as dawn.

From the look in the children's eyes, I might have descended from a spaceship. I gave Misha the presents my own son Jesse had picked out, bubble gum and baseball cards. Soon all three young jaws were chewing, all six small hands were shuffling through glossy photos of pitchers and sluggers.

Mrs. Filatova swept baby Ivan into her arms and crowed to him, "This is a once-in-a-century event, to have such a guest!"

Ivan gazed at me dubiously, then climbed into the stout arms of his grandfather, who cuddled and teased him while showing me around the homemade greenhouses and the garden. The black soil spoke exuberantly in carrots, tomatoes, radishes, beets. Climbing beans covered the arbor over the table where we would eat, at the back of the lot near the summer kitchen. Barrels at the corners of the roof caught rain water for washing. Lush vines hid melons and squash. Anise and dill spiced the air. I took pleasure in the vigor of the place and in the signs of labor. The savory food I had been eating all week had come from this dirt, these hands.

After a while I retired to the porch, hoping to write up some notes. Within moments the grandchildren crept in after me and stood at arm's length, staring. One by one they began speaking to me in Russian, even a few monosyllables from Ivan, then all of them chattered at once, unable to believe that a grown-up could not speak their language. Anya in particular kept firing questions, then waiting for answers with hands on hips and lovely saucer face cocked up at me. Misha, a rambunctious tow-head wearing a Mickey Mouse shirt, showed me a war scene he had sketched with a burning iron onto a plank, a scene of U.S. and Soviet troops battling Nazis. He pointed to a star on one of the American tanks and then to my chest. Allies. Mrs. Filatova came to shoo the children away, but as soon as she turned her back they materialized again, a circle of inquisitive eyes.

Riding his bike and clambering up trees and rollicking among the cottages with friends, Misha remained elusive all day, so that I had to observe him from a distance. "He is a very good boy," said Andrei, "but he will never be a diplomat. He is too honest. He says just what he thinks. He promises me that he will never, never lie. I say to him this is the important thing, for a man to be honest." At the end of the day, Misha would beg to return with us to Moscow. Marina would say no. It was not a good time. He was better off here in the country. In the car going home she would explain to me that some women, such as Lena, were content being mothers only, without jobs, but that other women, including herself, needed a career outside the family.

Far from being elusive, Anya adopted me. Slender like her aunt Marina, silky hair cut into bangs in front and dangling in a ponytail behind, she wore that day a blue polka-dot dress and white knee socks with red sneakers. When the family went for a saunter through the woods, Anya took my hand and led me gaily forward, only letting go to dash away and pluck a wildflower for me. She kept up a joyful prattle the whole time. Overhearing, Andrei laughed and said that Anya wanted to go back to America with me. Would she like to ride in my suitcase? I asked. Yes, came the reply, that would be fine. By the time we returned to the cottage for dinner, I had a fistful of wildflowers and a heartful of tenderness.

Over dinner, which began with mushrooms and caviar and proceeded through salmon, fish soup, platters of vegetables, chicken, watermelon, and pineapple, the Filatov clan joked and told stories. Sun filtering through the leaf-covered arbor bathed us in a minty light. Although the children were supposed to be eating in the summer kitchen, they kept slipping back to sit with the grown-ups. Ivan, babbling the universal baby language of "ba!" and "da!" was passed around the table. Anya plumped down beside me and thumbed through a deck of cards, teaching me the names and numbers in Russian, refusing to turn the next card until I had repeated the words to her satisfaction. (Andrei and Marina would later tell me they had feared that Anya, a cheeky little vixen, would act up during my visit, and that, alas, she had. Behavior they regarded as impolite struck me as enchanting.) Misha teasingly said he would tell Mr. Gorbachev on us, for drinking vodka! Mrs. Filatova drank along with the men, but Lena and Marina stuck with red Georgian wine. After three vodkas, Andrei shrugged and told me he could no longer speak English. Mr. Filatov said that after four vodkas, I would begin speaking Russian. As one who drinks wine seldom and vodka never, I now drank my fourth glass, and could barely speak any human language. Fortunately, I did not have to use my legs for a long while, because we sat talking for most of the afternoon. I told them how much I admired their family collective. Now they must have a cow and chickens! A cow, yes, said Mr. Filatov, and we shall put her front end in our neighbor's plot, where she can eat, and her rear end in our plot, where we can milk her! Let us do away with nuclear weapons, Andrei proposed. So that I may live here in peace with my beautiful women! Mr. Filatov cried. To understanding between our peoples! To prosperity! To love!

As we prepared to leave, Mrs. Filatova solemnly presented me with a bouquet of red zinnias, which I held gratefully all the way back to Moscow, warming myself at their blaze.

LENA CALLED MARINA before breakfast on Wednesday to say that all the neighboring cottagers were buzzing about the mysterious visit of the American. They were demanding to know how the Filatovs, out of all the millions of Soviet families, had been chosen for such an honor. Honor? I thought, sitting at the kitchen table in my jeans and ignorance.

"Marina is on the phone all the time," Andrei observed. "To her sister, her mother, her women friends."

"Only a few short calls each day," Marina replied testily after saying goodbye to Lena. "They are necessary for keeping our home. Someone must keep the home!"

There followed a dispute that was playful on the surface but serious underneath, Andrei claiming that Soviet women enjoy full equality with men, Marina insisting that, regardless of laws, women still do all the cooking, shopping, cleaning, washing, and most of the fretting over children. If more of our leaders were women, she claimed, perhaps we would have automatic clothes washers, dishwashers, prepared foods, shorter lines in the shops. If we are to do our work outside the home, we must have more help inside the home, from machines or men.

This was a woman whose colleagues and students at the Oil and Gas Institute were, to a person, male. This was a woman who knew that, the higher she rose, the fewer sisters there would be. This was a woman who kept a volume of Lenin open on the counter while she cooked, snatching moments to read. Washing dishes, a cloth in one hand and a plate in the other, she would speak about communism, capitalism, the Soviet future, not as abstractions but as palpable realities, her eyes alight.

"Marina is more disciplined than I am, more serious," Andrei admitted. "Me, I am drawn to many things, television and sports, the newspapers, mystery stories, long walks. Marina works hard. I try to help her. I buy bread. I order food at my work. I don't like to clean plates, but even that I have learned to do."

I asked how she had come to study philosophy. "When I was a teenager, many things in our lives I could not understand. There were contradictions between what was said and what I saw around me. So I wanted to find out the truth, to understand economics and so-

ciety. The task of a philosopher is to explain the world.
But first you must understand it yourself. That is why I
decided to study philosophy, beginning with the ancient
Greeks. I became a teacher in order to share this knowledge with students. I do not want them to imitate my
ideas, but to think for themselves, to find solutions for
our problems. I do not teach propaganda. I teach young
people how to think, so that we can make a better world,
so we can have more beauty in our lives."

"What sort of beauty?" I asked over the omelettes
and sliced peppers, above the ruckus of radio and television.

"I want our people to smile," Marina answered. "I
want to see them laugh, not only in their homes, but
on the streets, in the shops, in the factories. I want to
see joy in their faces."

"What would bring joy?"

"Abundance. The certainty of peace. True democracy. Individuals must have the power to influence society. The state must reflect the desires and imagination
of ordinary people."

Andrei declared soberly, "Fear must be eliminated
from our hearts. Lenin said that in our country the most
difficult task is for every man to kill slavery in his soul.
And Chekhov said the same before Lenin. It is a very
old need for us."

"Only think of Stalin," Marina said.

"It was not simply fear that kept people silent during
Stalin's reign of terror," said Andrei. "It was because he
declared that his way was Lenin's way. To disagree with
him was to go against Lenin, to become an enemy of the
people."

"I want Misha to grow up without fear," said Marina. "I want him to study humanities and foreign languages. I want him to travel freely around the world, to enjoy using his mind."

They planned for Misha to join the Young Pioneers at the age of ten ("so that he may learn to be moral, brave, and a true friend," said Andrei), and to join Komsomol, the Communist Youth League, at fourteen ("to learn about the vision of democracy").

"Then will he join the Party?" I asked.

"Misha will decide for himself," Andrei replied. "Marina and I joined in the period of Brezhnev—the time of *zastoy*, stagnation—because that was the only way to become involved in changing society."

"Now there are other ways, other avenues," Marina added.

Andrei said earnestly, "We are very lucky to be alive in this time, when the world is changing around us every day. We are lucky to be young in a time of revolution."

THE SOVIET REVOLUTION has continued in fits and starts for seven decades, a long time measured against the lifespan of an individual, but a short time measured against the life of Russian civilization. A few months before my visit, the Orthodox Church had celebrated the one thousandth anniversary of the arrival of Christianity in Russia. (Andrei made a point of telling me that the festivities had been covered respectfully on television and in the press: another sign of change.) In the years immediately following Red October of 1917, countless churches, monasteries, nunneries, and cathedrals were destroyed, and the destruction continued on through the reigns of Stalin and Khrushchev. Andrei grieved over each loss. As we journeyed through Moscow, he pointed out sites where religious buildings had been razed to make way for a monument, a warehouse, a swimming pool. "Although I am an atheist, I feel our history is bound up in the Church. Through all the invasions and wars, the Church preserved our manuscripts and art, the life of the spirit."

Despite the losses, enough ornate, onion-domed churches still survive in Moscow to give the city an ecclesiastical air. We never passed one without a comment from Andrei. Outside the gilded church of St. Nikolai, where we stopped Wednesday noon on our way to the archive, he said, "These treasures belong to all of us, believers and unbelievers alike. They speak of our past. We all believe in the spirit inside," he said, thumping his chest, "whether we call that spirit God or by some other name."

The presence of history came through to me powerfully on our tour of the Central State Archives for Historical Acts. Catherine the Great ordered the construction of the building two centuries ago, to store the records of imperial Russia. Our guide was the director, Mikhail Lukachev, dark-haired and intense, quite young at 37 to be a protector of the nation's memory. In his office, among bookshelves that reached to a high and shadowy ceiling, Mr. Lukachev showed me with almost religious fervor a number of the most valuable documents, his fingers hovering respectfully above the scrolls and jeweled books and illuminated manuscripts. Then he led me through the five floors of shelves, a maze of history, aisle upon aisle of brown boxes neatly labeled, and I imagined myself inside the convolutions of a brain. It seemed a sluggish yet potent brain, like that of a drowsing giant. In Andrei's department, half a dozen clerks were laboriously cataloguing the millions of documents by hand, writing in ink on stiff cards, without computers. Slow, slow, yet I had a sense in the archives, as everywhere else in Moscow, of a mind recovering from trauma, from partial amnesia, a mind beginning to reclaim its past.

Andrei felt linked to the past by way of his family, about which he told me that evening as we meandered through the old neighborhood called Arbat, vainly searching for a place to eat. Born in Moscow in 1955, an only child, Andrei had lived until the age of ten along with his parents and his maternal grandparents in one room of a three-bedroom apartment. Another pair of families occupied the other two bedrooms. "It was very, very difficult for us, but not unusual in those days." His mother traveled a good deal in connection with her work as a director's assistant for Mosfilm, the state cinema company. His father traveled constantly, driving trains. Thus Andrei was raised chiefly by his grandparents. The grandfather, a veteran of World War I, the October Revolution, and the Civil War, told him spellbinding tales of the gory and visionary beginnings of the Soviet Union. While serving his two years in the army as a paratrooper, Andrei was stationed in the northern city of Pskov. The grandfather wrote him a letter about having served there as a soldier himself, half a century earlier, in the war against the Kaiser. He also recounted being jailed under Stalin, losing his army commission, and emerging from prison to an uncertain life of odd jobs. Was the old man bitter? "No, he considered himself lucky to be alive. Many of his comrades died in Stalin's camps. He insisted that the *idea* of communism was just as valid, despite Stalin. He taught me that Stalin was the *deformation* of communism, a turning away from the true path laid out by Lenin."

Andrei had often told these and other family stories to Misha, who pleased him by retelling them to playmates. "Memories must be preserved in people, not only in books and movies. We must not lose history, because it teaches us who we are."

And so a day that began with talk about the Soviet future ended with talk about the past. The ligaments binding the one to the other, visible in the streets and buildings of Moscow, pass invisibly through consciousness. Andrei finished his family chronicle as we strolled by Pushkin Square, where clusters of gesturing men were talking politics. The square had recently become a rallying place for citizens eager to discuss the changes underway in their society. "You see, it is the question on everyone's mind: Where have we come from, where should we go?"

AFTER FEEDING ME luscious batter-fried eggplant, fresh from her father's garden, Marina asked me Thursday morning how American communists were viewed in our country.

"As anachronisms, liars, and hacks," I answered.

"We see them as robot servants of an alien power."

"It is because, for you, communism still means Stalinism?"

"For many of us."

Andrei turned from the kitchen window, where he always stood while smoking, in deference to Marina's dislike of the habit. He grimaced. "We are still trying to dig out from under Stalin."

Later in the day we toured the graveyard at the Novodevichy Nunnery, where many of the nation's famous and infamous are buried. Bright flowers had been heaped on the somber stones of Chekhov, Mayakovski, Gogol, on generals and cosmonauts, singers and scientists, film stars and scholars. Khrushchev's angular black and white marker had been designed, at his own request, by the avant-garde sculptor Ernst Neizvestny, whose works Khrushchev had condemned and who had been forced into exile. A solitary rose lay at the foot of the stone. "Few have anything good to say about Khrushchev today," Andrei murmured, "and yet he was the first to speak the truth about Stalin." Hundreds of people shuffled silently through the forested and ferny aisles, laying bouquets, fingering inscriptions, paying their respects to heroes and heroines. I have never known Americans to approach the dead so worshipfully. By far the largest crowd huddled beside the grave of Stalin's wife. Everyone and everything associated with the godlike ruler was still a potent lure. "Even now," Andrei whispered, "many people think back on him as a man of order, one who built up our strength, made the world respect us."

Family burial plots in less venerated Moscow cemeteries await Andrei and Marina. "We are deep-rooted

Muscovites, back several generations," Andrei explained with evident pride, "and so it is right for us to be planted at last in Moscow dirt."

After supper Thursday night we watched a television showing of *Agonia,* a film by Elem Klimov, about the religious fanatic Rasputin and the end of czarist rule. Made in 1976, the film had been "put on the shelf" because authorities feared that audiences would see parallels between the social paralysis under the last czar and the paralysis under Brezhnev. Only after Brezhnev's death and Gorbachev's rise to power, marking a dynamic new era, had the film been released. Andrei and Marina sat through it now a second time, never tiring of the steady diet of history.

That evening the radio played a new song, whose lyrics Andrei translated for me: A green shoot has broken through the roadway, splitting the stones of the old road, the road of tyranny, and we will never go that way again.

OVER COFFEE AND CHOCOLATES the next morning we spoke with shared melancholy of the distance that would soon separate us again. "You must not leave!" said Marina. "You must remain with us for another week."

"For a month," said Andrei.

"A year!" said Marina.

"Until you learn Russian!" Andrei boomed his laugh.

The Russian word *nemetz,* like the Greek root of *barbarian,* originally meant anyone whose speech was unintelligible, and thus an outsider, a presumed enemy. Today, *nemetz* means German. As we nibbled our chocolates, a documentary about German atrocities during the Great Patriotic War was playing on television. Strewn bodies, gutted buildings, grieving survivors. Twenty million dead. Perhaps thirty million, according to some estimates. All four of Andrei and Marina's grandfathers had fought in that war. One was killed by the Nazis, another died soon after from wartime trauma. The trauma still ran like a fissure through all our talk, through the streets of Moscow, across the kitchen table. The only memories of suffering I have encountered that rival this one for intensity are those of Jews remembering the holocaust and of blacks recalling slavery.

THE GRANDIOSE PARK on Moscow's north side, called the "Exhibition of the Economic Achievements of the U.S.S.R.," which we toured on Friday afternoon, celebrates the Soviet present and future. Airplanes, oil derricks, tractors: the heroism of machines. Yet even here I met with reminders of the painful past. Knowing of my interests, Andrei and Marina led me first to the exhibit on space exploration. Amid the towering rockets and intricate satellites, the object that moved me most deeply was the first Sputnik, a mirror-bright sphere about the size of a volleyball, bewhiskered with antennas, the symbol to me since my twelfth year of our power to reach into space. Next Marina showed me the flower pavilion—gladiolas, asters, zinnias, begonias, marigolds, all displayed against carpets of moss, feathery ferns, mottled philodendrons. Andrei meanwhile sat on a bench, muttering, "I am not a man of flowers."

Between pavilions, Marina bought us jam-filled doughnuts, orange soda, rolled-up waffles stuffed with cream. On my tongue the sweetness mingled with the bitterness of departure.

Our final stop was at a recently opened exhibit on the nation's history, ranging from medieval Russia to the modern Soviet Union. What struck me about the exhibit, and what captivated throngs of citizens who crowded around the glass cases, were the revelations about Stalin's terror. Case after case documented the lives of the millions who starved in keeping with Stalin's policies, the hundreds of thousands who were imprisoned and murdered, the countless lives broken by his mad whims. Under the title "Erased Names," Stalin-era photographs with faces blacked out were shown next to archival photographs with the faces restored. A history which had been lost from public view was becoming visible; a history known in bedrooms and whispered in kitchens was finally being proclaimed in the open air. Amid the throngs, Andrei and Marina pressed their faces to the glass and with taut lips read of their inheritance.

We emerged from the history exhibit into a misty rain that suited our mood. Marina gave one umbrella to Andrei, another to me. When I opened it, she gently took my arm and I felt blessed, as though a bird had settled there. While Andrei stood in line to buy cigarettes, Marina told me in halting but elegantly pronounced English that she hoped one day to write books, books that would illuminate some part of the world for her people. If she worked very hard, and if she was very fortunate, perhaps some day she would become a professor in a university. She tilted her valentine face at me, to see if I thought her dreams too grand. I smiled to show my confidence in her. The rain, the hand on my arm, the brave English, the confession of modest hopes, all together carried me to new depths of sympathy with this woman, her husband, their people.

WE TOOK REFUGE from the rain in an art gallery. Although abstract, surrealist, and expressionist works had recently been put on display in Moscow, after having been officially denounced for seventy years as bourgeois decadence, here all the paintings were conservative landscapes, village scenes, church domes outlined against sunsets. Having neither the space nor the money to carry back a painting, I asked my friends to advise me which of the small prints I should purchase, one I could hang on my wall at home to remember them by. After some deliberation, Andrei settled on a woodcut of workers and soldiers marching before a triumphal arch. "History!" he exclaimed. "The Soviet people!" No, Marina insisted, I should buy the ghostly moonlit scene of a farmhouse and pasture and trees. It reminded her of a childhood spent living in the country with a dear grandmother. "This will make you think of nature and the Russian earth," she said. They disagreed sharply, arguing for their respective visions: city and country, people and soil, human history and timeless nature, crowds and solitude. Both visions were true, so I purchased both prints. I look at the images now as I write, tiny windows onto that immense land.

From the gallery it was only a few steps to the Church of Ivan the Warrior, where we arrived in time for the Friday evening service. Built to commemorate a victory over Sweden in 1709, and thus another sign of the military current that flows through Russian history, the church is a compact jewel box, its varnished icons and gilded ornaments and sumptuous shrines reflecting light from hundreds of votive candles. As we stood in this glow, the church filled with elderly *babushkas*, then a few young women, a handful of men, and finally a clutch of children. The old women knelt, pressed fingers and foreheads and lips to the floor, elaborately crossing themselves, then rose on stiff knees to fondle shrines and kiss the golden frames of icons. What did my scientific materialist friends make of this spectacle? "Very beautiful, very strange," Andrei whispered. Without a word, Marina slipped away to light a candle. Returning, she pointed out to me high in the gleaming nave the icon of St. Mikhail, on whose day their son, Mikhail, was born. The boy had been christened, and so had she.

ON THE TENTH FLOOR of yet another apartment tower, this one built for employees of Mosfilm, we visited Andrei's parents, who fed us roasted duck and exuberant talk on Friday night. Mr. Svetenco was a booming man in his fifties, vigorous, stout, with an Abe Lincoln fringe of beard and a monkish circle of hair surrounding a polished scalp. A few years older (and by virtue of that the boss of the family, according to Andrei), Mrs. Svetenco was a plump woman with a big laugh, a small voice, and a smile that shone steadily from a face haloed by wispy gray hair.

The television, which burbled at one end of the table like an idiot guest all during supper, drove our conversation. The report of a chess tournament drew cries of dismay and approval from Andrei and his father. "Where are your great American chess players?" Mr. Svetenco demanded of me. News from the Republican convention, where George Bush had just been nominated, provoked a dispute between son and parents concerning the presidential candidates. News from Korea prompted Mr. Svetenco to ask if I thought the United States would win the upcoming Olympic Games. I told him I had no idea. "No idea? You don't care? Our athletes have been *ordered* to win. They must win for the nation!" Every topic was charged with politics, from Nicaragua to Afghanistan, books to medicine, cars to cartoons. Listening, I could hear in the Svetencos the same passionate engagement with the world that I had found in Andrei and Marina. In all the Soviets I met, there was a degree of political and cultural alertness that I have rarely encountered in Americans, an alertness gained from a lifetime of battles fought over their land, their cities, their homes, and their ideas.

After supper, I leafed through the family albums, studying photographs of Andrei from his first months up through school, Young Pioneers, Komsomol, the army, his courtship with Marina, their wedding, the birth of Misha. And then, with Misha's baby pictures, the cycle began repeating itself. I thought of waves forming offshore, rising to a crest, then breaking onto the sand, and new waves forming.

When it came time for us to leave, Mr. Svetenco rummaged through his collection of coins and presented me with a 1924 silver ruble, which shows a peasant and a worker set off against a grain field, factory, and rising

sun. "Do you know why the date is important?" Mr. Svetenco asked.

"Lenin died that year," I answered.

He slapped me on the back. I had passed a test.

Bidding us goodbye, Mrs. Svetenco lit up with her
beatific smile and uttered her favorite English phrases:
"Good evening! You are very kind! America is wonder-
ful!"

A KNIFE CLATTERED to the kitchen floor on Saturday
morning. Marina laughed. "To drop a knife means a man
will visit."

"And here is the man, but he is leaving!" Andrei
gestured at me with spread palms, as though handing me
a present.

The present they had been handing me all week,
even more precious than their company and food and
roof, was their trust. I reflected again on how much courage it took for them to accept this foreigner into their
home, without any script, without any notion of how I
would see their lives, how I would report their beliefs.
Andrei told me with amusement of several friends who
had been astonished that he and Marina would expose
themselves to such an unknown and potentially dangerous character. "An American! They say what you write
may get us in trouble!"

Writing has often brought trouble in the Soviet
Union, both for the writers and for those written about.
I knew the record only too well. It was encouraging to
see that Pasternak, Akhmatova, Bulgakov, and other

great writers of the Soviet era had recently been restored from oblivion, that censorship had been relaxed, that journals and newspapers were allowing for sharp differences of opinion. But how far would *glasnost* go? How long would it endure? Would it survive until after my report of Andrei and Marina's lives reached print?

OUR LAST ACT before leaving the apartment was to sit a few moments in silence. My friends explained that this is a Russian custom, to assure me a safe journey, a quick return, and a bond between our hearts while we are parted. Joined all week by talk, we were joined at last by silence.

At the airport, the clock forced me to pull away from their hugs. I passed through the first of the many barriers I would have to cross before reaching my own home. When I trusted myself to turn around, blinking at tears, it was too late, for I could not find their faces in the crowd.

On the plane, too numb to write, I leafed unheeding through a newspaper. English looked odd. As we taxied, the birches along the runway slipping by like needles of light against the somber firs, I came to a news item that seemed worth reading. It quoted the chief Soviet cartographer as saying that ever since the Revolution all maps of his country had been distorted for ideological reasons. Villages had been erased, towns and roads had been moved, the location of natural resources had been concealed, borders had been redrawn. Now the new regime was ordering him to draw up a true map. I read of this as we lifted off from Russian soil. Of course no map can be utterly true, since the world is richer than any image we make of it. No history, no record of a week spent with strangers in an alien city, no account of where we are and of how we reached this place can ever be complete. But some maps are more accurate than others, some histories truer. All history is a selective remembering. We are defined as nations and as individuals by what we do not forget.

III

PURPOSES

&

POWERS

THE
SINGULAR
FIRST PERSON

THE FIRST SOAPBOX ORATOR I EVER SAW WAS HARANGU-
ing a crowd beside the Greyhound Station in Provi-
dence, Rhode Island, about the evils of fluoridated
water. What the man stood on was actually an upturned
milk crate, all the genuine soapboxes presumably having
been snapped up by antique dealers. He wore an orange
plaid sports coat and matching bow tie and held aloft a
bottle filled with mossy green liquid. I don't remember
the details of his spiel, except his warning that fluoride
was an invention of the Communists designed to weaken
our bones and thereby make us pushovers for a Red invasion. What amazed me, as a tongue-tied kid of seventeen newly arrived in the city from the boondocks,
was not his message but his courage in delivering it to a

mob of strangers. I figured it would have been easier for me to jump straight over the Greyhound Station than to stand there on that milk crate and utter my thoughts.

To this day, when I read or when I compose one of those curious monologues we call the personal essay, I often think of that soapbox orator. Nobody had asked him for his two cents' worth, but there he was declaring it with all the eloquence he could muster. The essay, although enacted in private, is no less arrogant a performance. Unlike novelists and playwrights, who lurk behind the scenes while distracting our attention with the puppet show of imaginary characters, unlike scholars and journalists, who quote the opinions of others and shelter behind the hedges of neutrality, the essayist has nowhere to hide. While the poet can lean back on a several-thousand-year-old legacy of ecstatic speech, the essayist inherits a much briefer and skimpier tradition. The poet is allowed to quit after a few lines, but the essayist must hold our attention over pages and pages. It is a brash and foolhardy form, this one-man or one-woman circus, which relies on the tricks of anecdote, conjecture, memory, and wit to enthrall us.

ADDRESSING A MONOLOGUE to the world seems all the more brazen or preposterous an act when you consider what a tiny fraction of the human chorus any single voice is. At the Boston Museum of Science an electronic meter records with flashing lights the population of the United States. Figuring in the rate of births, deaths, emigrants leaving the country and immigrants arriving, the meter calculates that we add one fellow citizen every twenty-one seconds. When I looked at it recently, the count stood at 249,958,483. As I wrote that figure in my notebook, the final number jumped from three to four. Another mouth, another set of ears and eyes, another brain. A counter for the earth's population would stand somewhere past five billion at the moment, and would be rising in a blur of digits. Amid this avalanche of selves, it is a wonder that anyone finds the gumption to sit down and write one of those naked, lonely, quixotic letters-to-the-world.

A surprising number do find the gumption. In fact, I have the impression there are more essayists at work in America today, and more gifted ones, than at any time in recent decades. Whom do I have in mind? Here is a sampler: Wendell Berry, Carol Bly, Joan Didion, Annie Dillard, Stephen Jay Gould, Elizabeth Hardwick, Edward Hoagland, Phillip Lopate, Barry Lopez, Peter Matthiessen, John McPhee, Cynthia Ozick, Paul Theroux, Lewis Thomas, Tom Wolfe. No doubt you could make up a list of your own—with a greater ethnic range, perhaps, or fewer nature enthusiasts—a list that would provide equally convincing support for the view that we are blessed right now with an abundance of essayists. We do not have anyone to rival Emerson or Thoreau, but in sheer quantity of first-rate work our time stands comparison with any period since the heyday of the form in the mid-nineteenth century.

Why are so many writers taking up this risky form, and why are so many readers—to judge by the statistics of book and magazine publication—seeking it out? In this era of prepackaged thought, the essay is the closest thing we have, on paper, to a record of the individual mind at work and play. It is an amateur's raid in a world of specialists. Feeling overwhelmed by data, random information, the flotsam and jetsam of mass culture, we relish the spectacle of a single consciousness making sense of a portion of the chaos. We are grateful to Lewis Thomas for shining his light into the dark corners of biology, to John McPhee for laying bare the geology beneath our landscape, to Annie Dillard for showing us the universal fire blazing in the branches of a cedar, to Peter Matthiessen for chasing after snow leopards and mystical insights in the Himalayas. No matter if they are sketchy, these maps of meaning are still welcome. As Joan Didion observes in her own collection of essays, *The White Album*, "We live entirely, especially if we are writers, by the imposition of a narrative line upon disparate images, by the 'ideas' with which we have learned to freeze the shifting phantasmagoria which is our actual experience." Dizzy from a dance that seems to accelerate hour by hour, we cling to the narrative line, even though it may be as pure an invention as the shapes drawn by Greeks to identify the constellations.

The essay is a haven for the private, idiosyncratic voice in an era of anonymous babble. Like the bland-burgers served in their millions along our highways, most language served up in public these days is textureless, tasteless mush. On television, over the phone, in the newspaper, wherever humans bandy words about, we encounter more and more abstractions, more empty formulas. Think of the pablum ladled out by politicians. Think of the fluffy white bread of advertising. Think, lord help us, of committee reports. By contrast, the essay remains stubbornly concrete and particular: it confronts you with an oil-smeared toilet at the Sunoco station, a red vinyl purse shaped like a valentine heart, a bow-legged dentist hunting deer with an elephant gun. As Orwell forcefully argued, and as dictators seem to agree, such a bypassing of abstractions, such an insistence on the concrete, is a politically subversive act. Clinging to this door, that child, this grief, following the zigzag motions of an inquisitive mind, the essay renews language and clears trash from the springs of thought. A century and a half ago, in the rousing manifesto entitled *Nature*, Emerson called on a new generation of writers to cast off the hand-me-down rhetoric of the day, to "pierce this rotten diction and fasten words again to visible things." The essayist aspires to do just that.

As if all these virtues were not enough to account for a renaissance of this protean genre, the essay has also taken over some of the territory abdicated by contemporary fiction. Whittled down to the bare bones of plot, camouflaged with irony, muttering in brief sentences and grade-school vocabulary, peopled with characters who stumble like sleepwalkers through numb lives, today's fashionable fiction avoids disclosing where the author stands on anything. In the essay, you had better speak from a region pretty close to the heart or the reader will detect the wind of phoniness whistling through your hollow phrases. In the essay you may be caught with your pants down, your ignorance and sentimentality showing, while you trot recklessly about on one of your hobbyhorses. You cannot stand back from the action, as Joyce instructed us to do, and pare your fingernails. You cannot palm off your cockamamie notions on some hapless character.

To our list of the essay's contemporary attractions we

should add the perennial ones of verbal play, mental adventure, and sheer anarchic high spirits. To see how the capricious mind can be led astray, consider the foregoing paragraph, which drags in metaphors from the realms of toys, clothing, weather, and biology, among others. That is bad enough; but it could have been worse. For example, I began to draft a sentence in that paragraph with the following words: "More than once, in sitting down to beaver away at a narrative, felling trees of memory and hauling brush to build a dam that might slow down the waters of time. . . ." I had set out to make some innocent remark, and here I was gnawing down trees and building dams, all because I had let that *beaver* slip in. On this occasion I had the good sense to throw out the unruly word. I don't always, as no doubt you will have noticed. Whatever its more visible subject, an essay is also about the way a mind moves, the links and leaps and jigs of thought. I might as well drag in another metaphor—and another unoffending animal—by saying that each doggy sentence, as it noses forward into the underbrush of thought, scatters a bunch of rabbits that go bounding off in all directions. The essayist can afford to chase more of those rabbits than the fiction writer can, but fewer than the poet. If you refuse to chase any of them, and keep plodding along in a straight line, you and your reader will have a dull outing. If you chase too many, you will soon wind up lost in a thicket of confusion with your tongue hanging out.

THE PURSUIT OF MENTAL RABBITS was strictly forbidden by the teachers who instructed me in English composition. For that matter, nearly all the qualities of the personal essay, as I have been sketching them, violate the rules that many of us were taught in school. You recall we were supposed to begin with an outline and stick by it faithfully, like a train riding its rails, avoiding sidetracks. Each paragraph was to have a topic sentence pasted near the front, and these orderly paragraphs were to be coupled end-to-end like so many boxcars. Every item in those boxcars was to bear the stamp of some external authority, preferably a footnote referring to a thick book, although appeals to magazines and newspapers would do in a pinch. Our diction was to be formal, dignified, shunning the vernacular. Polysyllabic words derived from Latin were preferable to the blunt lingo of the streets. Metaphors were to be used only in emergencies, and no two of them were to be mixed. And even in emergencies we could not speak in the first person singular.

Already as a schoolboy, I chafed against those rules. Now I break them shamelessly, in particular the taboo against using the lonely capital *I*. Just look at what I'm doing right now. My speculations about the state of the essay arise, needless to say, from my own practice as reader and writer, and they reflect my own tastes, no matter how I may pretend to gaze dispassionately down on the question from a hot-air balloon. As Thoreau declares in his cocky manner on the opening page of *Walden*: "In most books the *I*, or first person, is omitted; in this it will be retained; that, in respect to egotism, is the main difference. We commonly do not remember that it is, after all, always the first person that is speaking. I should not talk so much about myself if there were anybody else whom I knew as well." True for the personal essay, it is doubly true for an essay about the essay: one speaks always and inescapably in the first person singular.

We could sort out essays along a spectrum according to the degree to which the writer's ego is on display— with John McPhee, perhaps, at the extreme of self-effacement, and Norman Mailer at the opposite extreme of self-dramatization. Brassy or shy, center stage or hanging back in the wings, the author's persona commands our attention. For the length of an essay, or a book of essays, we respond to that persona as we would to a friend caught up in a rapturous monologue. When the monologue is finished, we may not be able to say precisely what it was about, any more than we can draw conclusions from a piece of music. "Essays don't usually boil down to a summary, as articles do," notes Edward Hoagland, one of the least summarizable of companions, "and the style of the writer has a 'nap' to it, a combination of personality and originality and energetic loose ends that stand up like the nap of a piece of wool and can't be brushed flat" ("What I Think, What I Am"). We make assumptions about that speaking voice, assumptions we cannot validly make about the narrators in fiction. Only a sophomore is permitted to ask if Huckleberry Finn ever had any children; but even literary sophisticates wonder in print about Thoreau's love life, Montaigne's domestic arrangements, De Quincey's opium habit, Virginia Woolf's depression.

Montaigne, who not only invented the form but nearly perfected it as well, announced from the start that his true subject was himself. In his note "To the Reader" at the beginning of the *Essays*, he slyly proclaimed:

> I want to be seen here in my simple, natural, ordinary fashion, without straining or artifice; for it is myself that I portray. My defects will here be read to the life, and also my natural form, as far as respect for the public has allowed. Had I been placed among those nations which are said to live still in the sweet freedom of nature's first laws, I assure you I should very gladly have portrayed myself here entire and wholly naked.

A few pages after this disarming introduction, we are told of the Emperor Maximilian, who was so prudish about exposing his private parts that he would not let a servant dress him or see him in the bath. The Emperor went so far as to give orders that he be buried in his underdrawers. Having let us in on this intimacy about Maximilian, Montaigne then confessed that he himself, although "bold-mouthed," was equally prudish, and that "except under great stress of necessity or voluptuousness," he never allowed anyone to see him naked. Such modesty, he feared, was unbecoming in a soldier. But such honesty is quite becoming in an essayist. The very confession of his prudery is a far more revealing gesture than any doffing of clothes.

A curious reader will soon find out that the word *essay*, as adapted by Montaigne, means a trial or attempt. The Latin root carries the more vivid sense of a weighing out. In the days when that root was alive and green, merchants discovered the value of goods and alchemists discovered the composition of unknown metals by the use of scales. Just so the essay, as Montaigne was the first to show, is a weighing out, an inquiry into the value, meaning, and true nature of experience; it is a private experiment carried out in public. In each of three successive editions, Montaigne inserted new material into his essays without revising the old material. Often the new statements contradicted the original ones, but Montaigne let them stand, since he believed that the only consistent fact about human beings is their inconsistency. In a celebration called "Why Montaigne Is Not a Bore," Lewis Thomas has remarked of him that "He [was] fond of his mind, and affectionately entertained by everything in his head." Whatever Montaigne wrote about—and he wrote about everything under the sun: fears, smells, growing old, the pleasures of scratching—he weighed on the scales of his own character.

IT IS THE *singularity* of the first person—its warts and crotchets and turn of voice—that lures many of us into reading essays, and that lingers with us after we finish. Consider the lonely, melancholy persona of Loren Eiseley, forever wandering, forever brooding on our dim and bestial past, his lips frosty with the chill of the Ice Age. Consider the volatile, Dionysian persona of D. H. Lawrence, with his incandescent gaze, his habit of turning peasants into gods and trees into flames, his quick hatred and quicker love. Consider that philosophical farmer, Wendell Berry, who speaks with a countryman's knowledge and a deacon's severity. Consider E. B. White, with his cheery affection for brown eggs and dachshunds, his unflappable way of herding geese while the radio warns of an approaching hurricane.

E. B. White, that engaging master of the genre, a champion of idiosyncrasy, introduced his own volume of *Essays* by admitting the danger of narcissism:

> I think some people find the essay the last resort of the egoist, a much too self-conscious and self-serving form for their taste; they feel that it is presumptuous of a writer to assume that his little excursions or his small observations will interest the reader. There is some justice in their complaint. I have always been aware that I am by nature self-absorbed and egoistical; to write of myself to the extent I have done indicates a too great attention to my own life, not enough to the lives of others.

Yet the self-absorbed Mr. White was in fact a delighted observer of the world, and shared that delight with us. Thus, after describing memorably how a circus girl practiced her bareback riding in the leisure moments between shows ("The Ring of Time"), he confessed: "As a writing man, or secretary, I have always felt charged with the safekeeping of all unexpected items of worldly or unworldly enchantment, as though I might be held personally responsible if even a small one were to be lost." That may still be presumptuous, but it is a presumption turned outward on the creation.

This looking outward helps distinguish the essay from pure autobiography, which dwells more complacently on the self. Mass murderers, movie stars, sports heroes, Wall Street crooks, and defrocked politicians may blather on about whatever high jinks or low jinks made them temporarily famous, may chronicle their exploits, their diets, their hobbies, in perfect confidence that the public is eager to gobble up every least gossipy scrap. And the public, according to sales figures, generally is. On the other hand, I assume the public does not give a hoot about my private life. If I write of hiking up a mountain with my one-year-old boy riding like a papoose on my back, and of what he babbled to me while we gazed down from the summit onto the scudding clouds, it is not because I am deluded into believing that my baby, like the offspring of Prince Charles, matters to the great world. It is because I know the great world produces babies of its own and watches them change cloud-fast before its doting eyes. To make that climb up the mountain vividly present for readers is harder work than the climb itself. I choose to write about my experience not because it is mine, but because it seems to me a door through which others might pass.

On THAT COCKY FIRST PAGE of *Walden*, Thoreau justified his own seeming self-absorption by saying that he wrote the book for the sake of his fellow citizens, who kept asking him to account for his peculiar experiment by the pond. There is at least a sliver of truth to this, since Thoreau, a town character, had been invited more than once to speak his mind at the public lectern. Most of us, however, cannot honestly say the townspeople have been clamoring for our words. I suspect that all writers of the essay, even Norman Mailer and Gore Vidal, must occasionally wonder if they are egomaniacs. For the essayist, in other words, the problem of authority is inescapable. By what right does one speak? Why should anyone listen? The traditional sources of authority no longer serve. You cannot justify your words by appealing to the Bible or some other holy text, you cannot merely stitch together a patchwork of quotations from classical authors, you cannot lean on a podium at the Atheneum and deliver your wisdom to a rapt audience.

In searching for your own soapbox, a sturdy platform from which to deliver your opinionated monologues, it helps if you have already distinguished yourself at some other, less fishy form. When Yeats describes his longing for Maud Gonne or muses on Ireland's misty lore, everything he says is charged with the prior strength of his poetry. When Virginia Woolf, in A Room of One's Own, reflects on the status of women and the conditions necessary for making art, she speaks as the author of Mrs. Dalloway and To the Lighthouse. The essayist may also lay claim to our attention by having lived through events or traveled through terrains that already bear a richness of meaning. When James Baldwin writes his Notes of a Native Son, he does not have to convince us that racism is a troubling reality. When Barry Lopez takes us on a meditative tour of the far north in Arctic Dreams, he can rely on our curiosity about that fabled and forbidding place. When Paul Theroux climbs aboard a train and invites us on a journey to some exotic destination, he can count on the romance of railroads and the allure of remote cities to bear us along.

Most essayists, however, cannot draw on any source of authority from beyond the page to lend force to the page itself. They can only use language to put themselves on display and to gesture at the world. When Annie Dillard tells us in the opening lines of *Pilgrim at Tinker Creek* about the tomcat with bloody paws who jumps through the window onto her chest, why should we listen? Well, because of the voice that goes on to say: "And some mornings I'd wake in daylight to find my body covered with paw prints in blood; I looked as though I'd been painted with roses." Listen to her explaining a few pages later what she is up to in this book, this broody, zestful record of her stay in the Roanoke Valley: "I propose to keep here what Thoreau called 'a meteorological journal of the mind,' telling some tales and describing some of the sights of this rather tamed valley, and exploring, in fear and trembling, some of the unmapped dim reaches and unholy fastnesses to which those tales and sights so dizzyingly lead." The sentence not only describes the method of her literary search, but also exhibits the breathless, often giddy, always eloquent and spiritually hungry soul who will do the searching. If you enjoy her company, you will relish Annie Dillard's essays; if you don't, you won't.

Listen to another voice which readers tend to find either captivating or insufferable:

That summer I began to see, however dimly, that one of my ambitions, perhaps my governing ambition, was to belong fully to this place, to belong as the thrushes and the herons and the muskrats belonged, to be altogether at home here. That is still my ambition. But now I have come to see that it proposes an enormous labor. It is a spiritual ambition, like goodness. The wild creatures belong to the place by nature, but as a man I can belong to it only by understanding and by virtue. It is an ambition I cannot hope to succeed in wholly, but I have come to believe that it is the most worthy of all.

That is Wendell Berry in "The Long-Legged House" writing about his patch of Kentucky. Once you have heard that stately, moralizing, cherishing voice, laced through with references to the land, you will not mistake it for anyone else's. Berry's themes are profound and arresting ones. But it is his voice, more than anything he speaks about, that either seizes us or drives us away.

Even so distinct a persona as Wendell Berry's or Annie Dillard's is still only a literary fabrication, of course. The first person singular is too narrow a gate for the whole writer to squeeze through. What we meet on the page is not the flesh-and-blood author, but a simulacrum, a character who wears the label *I*. Introducing the lectures that became *A Room of One's Own*, Virginia Woolf reminded her listeners that "'I' is only a convenient term for somebody who has no real being. Lies will flow from my lips, but there may perhaps be some truth mixed up with them; it is for you to seek out this truth and to decide whether any part of it is worth keeping." Here is a part I consider worth keeping: "Women have served all these centuries as looking-glasses possessing the magic and delicious power of reflecting the figure of man at twice its natural size." It is from such elegant, revelatory sentences that we build up our notion of the "I" who speaks to us under the name of Virginia Woolf.

WHAT THE ESSAY TELLS US may not be true in any sense that would satisfy a court of law. As an example, think of Orwell's brief narrative, "A Hanging," which describes an execution in Burma. Anyone who has read it remembers how the condemned man as he walked to the gallows stepped aside to avoid a puddle. That is the sort of haunting detail only an eyewitness should be able to report. Alas, biographers, those zealous debunkers, have recently claimed that Orwell never saw such a hanging, that he reconstructed it from hearsay. What then do we make of his essay? Or has it become the sort of barefaced lie we prefer to call a story?

Frankly, I don't much care what label we put on "A Hanging"—fiction or nonfiction, it is a powerful statement either way—but Orwell might have cared a great deal. I say this because not long ago I was bemused and then vexed to find one of my own essays treated in a scholarly article as a work of fiction. Here was my earnest report about growing up on a military base, my heartfelt rendering of indelible memories, being confused with the airy figments of novelists! To be sure, in writing the piece I had used dialogue, scenes, settings, character descriptions, the whole fictional bag of tricks; sure, I picked and chose among a thousand beckoning details; sure, I downplayed some facts and highlighted others; but I was writing about the actual, not the invented. I shaped the matter, but I did not make it up.

To explain my vexation, I must break another taboo, which is to speak of the author's intent. My teachers warned me strenuously to avoid the intentional fallacy. They told me to regard poems and plays and stories as objects washed up on the page from some unknown and unknowable shores. Now that I am on the other side of the page, so to speak, I think quite recklessly of intention all the time. I believe that if we allow the question of intent in the case of murder, we should allow it in literature. The essay is distinguished from the short story, not by the presence or absence of literary devices, not by tone or theme or subject, but by the writer's stance toward the material. In composing an essay about what it was like to grow up on that military base, I *meant* something quite different from what I mean when concocting a story. I meant to preserve and record and help give voice to a reality that existed independently of me. I meant to pay my respects to a minor passage of history in an out-of-the-way place. I felt responsible to the truth as known by other people. I wanted to speak directly out of my own life into the lives of others.

You can see I am teetering on the brink of metaphysics. One step farther and I will plunge into the void, wondering as I fall how to prove there is any external truth for the essayist to pay homage to. I draw back from the brink and simply declare that I believe one writes, in essays, with a regard for the actual world, with a respect for the shared substance of history, the autonomy of other lives, the being of nature, the mystery and majesty of a creation we have not made.

When it comes to speculating about the creation, I

feel more at ease with physics than with metaphysics. According to certain bold and lyrical cosmologists, there is at the center of black holes a geometrical point, the tiniest conceivable speck, where all the matter of a collapsed star has been concentrated, and where everyday notions of time, space, and force break down. That point is called a singularity. The boldest and most poetic theories suggest that anything sucked into a singularity might be flung back out again, utterly changed, somewhere else in the universe. The lonely first person, the essayist's microcosmic "I," may be thought of as a verbal singularity at the center of the mind's black hole. The raw matter of experience, torn away from the axes of time and space, falls in constantly from all sides, undergoes the mind's inscrutable alchemy, and reemerges in the quirky, unprecedented shape of an essay.

Now it is time for me to step down, before another metaphor seizes hold of me, before you notice that I am standing, not on a soapbox, but on the purest air.

Speaking

a Word

for Nature

WHY IS SO MUCH RECENT AMERICAN FICTION SO BAR-
ren? Putting the question more honestly, why do I find
myself reading fewer contemporary novels and stories
each year, and why do I so often feel that the work most
celebrated by literary mavens (both avant-garde and establishment) is the shallowest? What is missing? Clearly
there is no lack of verbal skill, nor of ingenuity in the
use of forms. And there is no shortage of writers: if you
pause in the checkout line at the supermarket the clerk
is likely to drag his manuscript from under the counter
and ask your opinion. It is as though we had an ever-
growing corps of wizards concocting weaker and weaker
spells.

To suggest what is missing, I begin with a passage from D. H. Lawrence's essay about Thomas Hardy. Lawrence argued that the controlling element in *The Return of the Native* is not the human action, but the setting where that action takes place, the wasteland of Egdon Heath: "What is the real stuff of tragedy in the book? It is the Heath. It is the primitive, primal earth, where the instinctive life heaves up. . . . Here is the deep, black source from whence all these little contents of lives are drawn." Lawrence went on to generalize:

> This is a constant revelation in Hardy's novels: that there exists a great background, vital and vivid, which matters more than the people who move upon it. Against the background of dark, passionate Egdon, of the leafy, sappy passion and sentiment of the woodlands, of the unfathomed stars, is drawn the lesser scheme of lives. . . . The vast, unexplored morality of life itself, what we call the immorality of nature, surrounds us in its eternal incomprehensibility, and in its midst goes on the little human morality play . . . seriously, portentously, till some one of the protagonists chances to look out of the charmed circle . . . into the wilderness raging round.

Every work of literature is the drawing of a charmed circle, since we can write about only a piece of the world. Within that circle, language shines meaning onto gestures, whispers, images, and objects. All the while, beyond our words, the universe cycles on. Much contemporary fiction seems to me barren in part because it draws such tiny, cautious circles, in part because it pretends that nothing lies beyond its timid boundaries. Such fiction treats some "little human morality play" as the whole of reality, and never turns outward to acknowledge the "wilderness raging round." And by wilderness I mean quite literally the untrammeled being of nature, which might include—depending on where you look—a woods, a river, an alien planet, the genetic code, a cloud of subatomic particles, or a cluster of galaxies. What is missing from much recent fiction, I feel, is any sense of nature, any acknowledgment of a nonhuman context.

While Lawrence's account seems to me largely true of Hardy, it does not apply to the mainstream of British fiction. In the work of British novelists from Defoe and Fielding through Austen, Dickens, George Eliot, Joyce, and Woolf, up to contemporaries such as Margaret Drabble and Anthony Powell, the social realm—the human morality play—is a far more powerful presence than nature. What Lawrence wrote about Hardy applies more widely and deeply, in fact, to American literature. Hardy glimpsed "the primitive, primal earth" in Dorset, and Wordsworth searched for it in the Lake District, and Lawrence himself found remnants of it amid the coal fields of the industrial Midlands. But these were pockets of wildness surrounded by a domesticated landscape. In America, by contrast, until well into this century—and even, in some desert and mountainous places, still today—writers have not had to hunt for wildness. For over three centuries, from the time of William Bradford in Plymouth Plantation to William Faulkner in Mississippi, when our writers looked outward from the circle of human activity, they could not help but see "the wilderness raging round." Our feelings toward this wild arena have shifted back and forth between a sense of revulsion as in Bradford and a sense of reverence as in Faulkner; but what has been constant through all except the last few decades of our history is the potent fact of the wilderness itself. Again and again in the great works of American literature, the human world is set against the overarching background of nature. As in Hardy's novels, this landscape is no mere scenery, no flimsy stage set, but rather the energizing *medium* from which human lives emerge and by which those lives are bounded and measured.

Soon after writing his essay on Hardy, Lawrence undertook a study of American literature, attracted by the same quality he had identified in *The Return of the Native*. In the works of Melville, Cooper, Hawthorne, Crèvecoeur, and Thoreau he found a divided consciousness: on the surface they were concerned with the human world, with towns and ships and cultivated land, with households and the spiderwebs of families; but underneath they were haunted by nature. Thus Melville seemed to Lawrence "more spell-bound by the strange slidings and collidings of Matter than by the things men do." Cooper sentimentalized the New York frontier in his Leatherstocking tales, yet wildness kept breaking through. This divided consciousness arose, Lawrence argued, because in America "there is too much menace in the landscape."

By the time his *Studies in Classic American Literature* (1923) appeared, Lawrence had moved to a ranch in New Mexico, and he could write from direct experience that, "when one comes to America, one finds . . . there is always a certain slightly devilish resistance in the . . . landscape." In *St. Mawr* (1925), a short novel written during his American stay, the heroine flees from England, where every scrap of country has been "humanized, occupied by the human claim;" and she settles as Lawrence did on a mountain overlooking the desert. Here she "felt a certain latent holiness in the very atmosphere . . . such as she had never felt in Europe, or in the East. . . . The landscape lived, and lived as the world of the gods, unsullied and unconcerned. . . . Man did not exist for it." Something like Lawrence's awestruck encounter with the American landscape has been recorded time and again in our literature. By sampling this tradition, we can see more vividly the sort of nature-awareness that has largely disappeared from contemporary fiction.

THE RESPONSE TO LAND as holy, as a source of meaning and energy, while it is an ancient view among Native Americans, is a fairly recent view for people of European descent. The earliest responses to the wilderness were typically those of horror and revulsion. Here, for example, is William Bradford, writing sometime after 1620 about the Pilgrims' first impression of their new land:

> [W]hat could they see but a hideous and desolate wilderness, full of wild beasts and wild men. . . . [W]hich way soever they turned their eyes (save upward to the heavens) they could have little solace or content in respect of any outward objects. . . . [A]ll things stand upon them with a weatherbeaten face,

and the whole country, full of woods and thickets, represented a wild and savage hue. If they looked behind them, there was the mighty ocean which they had passed and was now a main bar and gulf to separate them from all the civil parts of the world. (*Of Plymouth Plantation*)

One feels that in Bradford's devout eyes the wilderness was, if anything, more certain a presence than heaven itself. Merely because a writer is overwhelmingly *aware* of the American landscape, however, is no guarantee that he or she will know what to make of it. None of the intellectual gear that Bradford had carried with him from "the civil parts of the world," least of all his Puritan theology, had equipped him to see this New World with any clarity. Like many who followed in his religious tradition, including Hawthorne two centuries later, Bradford looked at the wilderness and saw the *un*holy, the *dis*ordered. It was all a menacing blur.

Since the time of Bradford, many of our writers—reluctant or unable to invent a fresh language of nature—have tried to squeeze American landscape into a European frame. Washington Irving, for example, taking a tour of the prairies in 1835 shortly after his return from a stay in Europe, described the Oklahoma frontier in terms of classical mythology, royal gardens, and French and Dutch painting. He laid out the countryside as if on canvas, with dark bands of trees or prairie in the foreground, lighter river valley or hills in the middle ground, and hazy sky in the distance, the whole suffused, as he remarked at one point, with "the golden tone of one of the landscapes of Claude Lorraine." The western forests

reminded him of Gothic cathedrals, "those vast and venerable piles, and the sound of the wind sweeping through
them supplie[d] the deep breathings of the organ." Later
in his account of the frontier expedition, Irving made
his Old World frame explicit:

> The prairies bordering on the rivers are always varied
> in this way with woodland, so beautifully interspersed
> as to appear to have been laid out by the hand of
> taste; and they only want here and there a village
> spire, the battlements of a castle, or the turrets of an
> old family mansion rising from among the trees, to
> rival the most ornamented scenery of Europe.

The "hand of taste" is evident here and throughout *A
Tour on the Prairies*, rearranging the rude Oklahoma
countryside to make it more nearly conform to the landscape of England or France.

Irving was only one in a long line of American writers who gazed at the wild countryside and regretted the
absence of human "ornament." Even so keen an observer
of our landscape as Thomas Cole voiced a complaint
similar to Irving's after returning (in 1832) from his own
European sojourn: "Although American scenery is often
so fine, we feel the want of associations such as cling to
scenes in the old world. Simple nature is not quite suf-
ficient. We want human interest, incident and action to
render the effect of landscape complete." Half a century
later, in a notorious essay on Hawthorne, Henry James
listed all the ornaments that were missing from the
American scene. It is a long list, including castles and
kings. By comparison with the Old World, the New had

little to offer except raw nature. And James had no more idea than Bradford what to make of a wild landscape. He felt at ease only in Europe, where nature had long since been cut into a human quilt. Still today, although young writers may no longer feel compelled to live in Paris or London, most who grow up in the backwoods or on the prairies—in Oklahoma, say, or Indiana—eventually pack their bags and head for the cities of the East Coast or the West, as if the land in between were too poor to support crops of literature.

While some writers were trying to squeeze New World landscapes into Old World frames, others tried to discover a fresh way of seeing the "primitive, primal earth" that was laid bare in America. One of the earliest inventors of this homegrown vision was William Bartram, the vagabond naturalist, who gazed at the American countryside on the eve of the Revolution. Here is Bartram reporting in his *Travels* about life in a Florida swamp:

> The verges and islets of the lagoon were elegantly embellished with flowering plants and shrubs; the laughing coots with wings half spread were tripping over the little coves, and hiding themselves in the tufts of grass; young broods of the painted summer teal, skimming the surface of the waters, and following the watchful parent unconscious of danger, were frequently surprised by the voracious trout; and he, in turn, as often by the subtle greedy alligator. Behold him rushing forth from the flags and reeds. His enormous body swells. His plaited tail brandished high, floats upon the lake. The waters like a cataract de-

scend from his opening jaws. Clouds of smoke issue from his dilated nostrils. The earth trembles with his thunder.

Darwin would not have had much to teach this intrepid naturalist on the subject of violence in nature. Despite these dragonlike alligators with their smoking nostrils, Bartram stuck around long enough to explore the swamps. Everywhere on his travels he learned what he could of the Indians, plants, soils, and beasts. He was helping, in fact, to invent scientific observation, a way of seeing and speaking of nature as separate, orderly, obedient to its own laws. He treated the lagoons and rivers and forests through which he traveled as a sequence of habitats, although of course he did not use that newfangled word.

Much of what Bartram saw astonished him, and he frequently had to grope for language—as when he came upon a run of fish at the mouth of a river:

> How shall I express myself so as to convey an adequate idea of it to the reader, and at the same time avoid raising suspicions of my veracity? Should I say, that the river . . . from shore to shore, and perhaps near half a mile above and below me, appeared to be one solid bank of fish, of various kinds . . . and that the alligators were in such incredible numbers, and so close together . . . that it would have been easy to have walked across on their heads, had the animals been harmless? What expressions can sufficiently declare the shocking scene that for some minutes continued, whilst this mighty army of fish were forcing the pass?

The American wilderness fed William Bartram a steady diet of surprise. He did not bemoan the absence of "human ornament," but on the contrary he celebrated the New World's teeming landscape.

The works of Bartram circulated widely in Europe, where a new generation of writers, including Wordsworth, Coleridge, and Chateaubriand, feeling encumbered by civilization, were eager for these glimpses of wild and wondrous territory. What often happened to American literary landscapes when they were transported across the ocean may be suggested by looking at Chateaubriand's New World romance, *Atala* (1801). Unlike most European Romantics, Chateaubriand actually traveled to America, spending the winter of 1791–92 in upstate New York. Not content to write about the landscape he had actually seen, however, he borrowed heavily from Bartram's *Travels* and from his own fancy to produce descriptions such as this one, of the Mississippi River:

> [W]hile the middle current sweeps the dead pines and oaks to the sea, one can see, on the side currents, floating isles of pistia and water lilies, whose pinkish yellow flowers, rising like little banners, are carried along the river banks. Green serpents, blue herons, pink flamingoes, young crocodiles sail like passengers on the flower-ships, and the colony, unfolding its golden sails to the wind, lazily drifts into some hidden bend of the river.

The bend must have been very well hidden, since no other traveler on the Mississippi has ever discovered a

scene remotely like that one. Along those fabulous
shores, the Frenchman noted mountains, Indian pyramids, caribou, bears drunk on grapes, and snakes that
disguised themselves as vines to catch birds. While Bartram was given to exaggeration, especially in the vicinity
of alligators, he always checked his enthusiasm against
what his eyes were telling him; Chateaubriand suffered
no such inhibitions.

Like Lawrence and many other European writers,
Chateaubriand was lured to America by the very qualities in our landscape that drove Cooper, Irving, and
James to Europe. This contrary movement has been
going on now for two centuries. I imagine that right this
minute, in the air over the Atlantic, jumbo jets are
crossing paths, the eastbound ones carrying Americans
to Europe in search of castles and gravestones, the west-
bound ones carrying Europeans to America in search of
redwoods and waterfalls.

Emerson had a look at landscapes on both sides of
the ocean, and decided that the native variety was the
one best suited to his imagination. His *Nature* (1836)
seems to me still the most eloquent manifesto for a way
of seeing appropriate to the New World setting. In the
essay he urged American writers to cast off the conven-
tions of thought inherited from Europe, that stuffy old ward-
robe of hand-me-down ideas, and "to look at the world
with new eyes." But how? By turning away from "the
artificial and curtailed life of cities" and going back to
the source of all thought and language, to nature itself:

> Hundreds of writers may be found in every long-civ-
> ilized nation, who for a short time believe, and make

others believe, that they see and utter truths, who do not of themselves clothe one thought in its natural garment, but who feed unconsciously on the language created by the primary writers of the country, those, namely, who hold primarily on nature. But wise men pierce this rotten diction and fasten words again to visible things.

This advice is easier to accept than to apply, as Emerson's own verbal landscapes demonstrate. In *Nature* itself, whenever he began to fasten words onto visible things—seeing, for instance, "The leafless trees become spires of flame in the sunset, with the blue east for their background, and the stars of the dead calices of flowers, and every withered stem and stubble rimed with frost,"—he interrupted himself to ask a question or to drag in some of that discarded European baggage: "What was it that nature would say? Was there no meaning in the live repose of the valley behind the mill, and which Homer or Shakespeare could not re-form for me in words?" Listening for what nature had to say, Emerson was always a little too eager to hear the cultural mutterings of his own well-stocked mind, and thus his landscapes are less substantial than those drawn by many of the writers who followed his precepts—including, most famously, Thoreau.

However much we might quarrel about who belongs on the short list of primary writers—those who renew our language and vision by fastening words to nature—I hope we would agree to include the name of Thoreau. His descriptions of the Concord River, the Maine woods, Cape Cod, and Walden Pond are among the most vigorous and penetrating accounts of our landscape ever written. One of his prime motives for undertaking the experiment in living beside Walden Pond was to train himself to *see*: "It is something to be able to paint a particular picture, or to carve a statue, and so to make a few objects beautiful; but it is far more glorious to carve and paint the very atmosphere and medium through which we look." In passage after passage of *Walden*, Thoreau portrayed a dynamic nature—frozen sand melting and sliding down the railroad embankment, ice breaking up on the pond, geese circling overhead and muskrats burrowing underfoot. Watching this energetic landscape was his chief business:

> Sometimes, in a summer morning, having taken my accustomed bath, I sat in my sunny doorway from sunrise till noon, rapt in a revery, amidst the pines and hickories and sumachs, in undisturbed solitude and stillness, while the birds sang around or flitted noiseless through the house, until by the sun falling in at my west window, or the noise of some traveller's wagon on the distant highway, I was reminded of the lapse of time. I grew in those seasons like corn in the night, and they were far better than any work of the hands would have been.

Thoreau situated himself *within* nature, and drew upon all the senses—he devoted an entire chapter of *Walden* to sounds, for example—to convey what was going on around him in the green world. The forces at work in pond and forest he found also at work in himself. An entry in his journal catches this feeling memorably: "A writer, a man writing, is the scribe of all nature; he is the corn and the grass and the atmosphere writing."

In Thoreau we find no conflict between the scientist's method of close, reasoned observation and the poet's free play of imagination. Since Thoreau's time, however, as the products of reason have come to dominate and efface the natural landscape, writers have found it more and more difficult to combine these two ways of seeing. In *Life on the Mississippi* (1883), for example, Samuel Clemens wrote about having to learn every mile of the shifting river by heart. He studied hard, and eventually became a professor of the river, but at a price:

> Now when I had mastered the language of this water and had come to know every trifling feature that bordered the great river as familiarly as I knew the letters of the alphabet, I had made a valuable acquisition. But I had lost something, too. I had lost something which could never be restored to me while I lived. All the grace, the beauty, the poetry had gone out of the majestic river!

However, we can see from *Adventures of Huckleberry Finn* (1885), published two years after *Life on the Mississippi*, that he was in fact able to fuse an adult's rational knowledge and a child's fresh emotion in his vision of the river. Here is Huck, for example, watching the sun rise over the Mississippi:

> The first thing to see, looking away over the water, was a kind of dull line—that was the woods on t'other

side—you couldn't make nothing else out; then a pale place in the sky; then more paleness, spreading around; then the river softened up, away off, and warn't black any more . . . and you see the mist curl up off of the water, and the east reddens up, and the river, and you make out a log cabin in the edge of the woods . . . then the nice breeze springs up, and comes fanning you from over there, so cool and fresh, and sweet to smell, on account of the woods and the flowers . . . and next you've got the full day, and everything smiling in the sun, and the song-birds just going it!

To sustain this vision of nature unsullied, Clemens had to push his narrative back into the time of his own childhood, some forty years earlier.

Faulkner did something similar in his novella, "The Bear." Although written near the beginning of World War II, it deals with events from a time sixty years earlier, when patches of wilderness still lingered in Mississippi. In order to see Old Ben, the fabled bear, Faulkner's young hero must leave behind his gun, his compass, his watch, every mechanical contrivance, and yield himself to the woods. At length he is granted his vision:

Then he saw the bear. It did not emerge, appear: it was just there, immobile, fixed in the green and windless noon's hot dappling, not as big as he had dreamed it but as big as he had expected, bigger, dimensionless against the dappled obscurity, looking at him. Then it moved. It crossed the glade without haste, walking for an instant into the sun's full glare and out of it, and stopped again and looked back at him across one shoulder. Then it was gone. It didn't walk into the woods. It faded, sank back into the wilderness without motion as he had watched a fish, a huge old bass, sink back into the dark depths of its pool and vanish without even any movement of its fins.

In the course of the novel Old Ben is killed, the last of the half-Indian hunters dies, and the stand of virgin timber is sold to lumber companies and invaded by railroads and whittled away by the surrounding farms. Faulkner was concerned in "The Bear" not so much with the conflict between reason and imagination in our ways of seeing nature, as with reason's wholesale assault upon nature itself. His fable reminds us that, in a little over a century, our wilderness continent was transformed into one of the most highly industrialized landscapes in the world.

AND THUS WE COME, by way of a far too sketchy history, to our own time. In an age of strip mines, nuclear plants, urban sprawl, interstate highways, factory farms, chemical dumps, mass extinction of plant and animal species, oil spills, and "development" of the few remaining scraps of wilderness, many of us have come to view our situation in a manner exactly contrary to that of William Bradford. The landscapes that we ourselves have fashioned often appear "hideous and desolate." We can no longer cut ourselves off from the "civil parts of the world," however much we might wish to.

What has become of nature in recent American writing? A decent answer would be longer than this entire essay, and even then could merely touch on a few literary landscapes—Wendell Berry's Kentucky, say, and Eudora Welty's Mississippi, the Roanoke Valley of Annie Dillard, Edward Hoagland's Vermont, John McPhee's Alaska, Thomas McGuane's Montana, the deserts of Edward Abbey and Barry Lopez, the alien planets of Ursula K. Le Guin, the Africa and Nepal of Peter Matthiessen, the great plains of N. Scott Momaday and Wright Morris, the fabulous Antarctic of John Calvin Batchelor and the Central American jungle of Paul Theroux, the microscopic arenas of Lewis Thomas. All of these writers seek to understand our life as continuous with the life of nature; they project "the little human morality play" against the "wilderness raging round."

Notice that most of them work outside the braided literary currents that critics, reviewers, and publishers regard as the "mainstream" of contemporary fiction. They work in the essay (Abbey, Lopez, Hoagland, McPhee, Dillard, Thomas); in science fiction or fantasy or fable (all of Le Guin, Batchelor's *The Birth of the People's Republic of Antarctica*, Theroux's *The Mosquito Coast*); in travel writing (Matthiessen, Theroux); or in "regional" fiction (meaning, so far as I can tell, fiction set in a recognizable landscape that is not a city: Berry, Welty).

Consider one brief example that stands for a larger pattern. Bobbie Ann Mason's *Shiloh and Other Stories* and the revision of Wendell Berry's *A Place on Earth* came out within a year of one another (1982 and 1983, respectively). Both are set in western Kentucky; both dwell on the breakup of rural lifeways. For Mason, nature supplies an occasional metaphor to illustrate a character's dilemma—a tulip tree cut down when it was about to bloom, a rabbit with crushed legs on the highway—exactly as K-Mart or Cat Chow or the Phil Donohue Show supply analogues. For Berry, no matter how much the land has been neglected or abused, no matter how ignorant of their environment people may have become, nature is the medium in which life transpires, a prime source of values and meaning and purpose. Whereas *Shiloh and Other Stories* was widely praised and imitated and briskly sold, *A Place on Earth*—a far more searching and eloquent book—was generally neglected; when reviewed at all, it was treated as an old-fashioned view of an out-of-the-way place.

That a deep awareness of nature has been largely excluded from "mainstream" fiction is a measure of the narrowing and trivialization of that fashionable current. It is also, of course, and more dangerously, a measure of a shared blindness in the culture at large. Not long ago, while camping in the Great Smoky Mountains, I had a nightmare glimpse of the modern reader. It was late one afternoon in May, the air sweet and mild. I left my tent and crossed the parking lot of the campground on my way to a cliff, where I planned to sit with my legs dangling over the brink and stare out across the westward mountains at the sunset. Already the sky was throbbing with color and the birds were settling down for their evening song. The wind smelled of pines. Near the center of the parking lot, as far as possible from the encircling trees, a huge camping van squatted. There were chocks under the tires, but the motor was running. The air-conditioner gave a high frantic squeal. The van had enough windows for a hothouse, but every one was curtained, even the windshield. Lights glowed around the edges and threw yellow slashes onto the blacktop. What could keep the passengers shut up inside that box on such an afternoon, in such a place? Passing by, I saw through a gap in the curtains a family clustered in front of a television as if in front of a glowing hearth, and I heard the unmistakable banshee cry of Tarzan, King of the Apes.

Whenever I am feeling gloomy about the prospects of making nature *present* to contemporary readers, I think of those campers. They had driven their rolling house to a mountaintop overlooking a glorious sweep of land, and had parked there, with engine running and curtains drawn, to watch a movie starring an Olympic swimmer playing an English lord swinging through a Hollywood jungle. If the Great Smoky Mountains could not lure them from their box, how could words on a page ever stir them? Could such people be made to see, through stories, where it is we actually dwell, what sort of ship we ride through space?

Of course, readers have always been willing to pull on their mental boots and journey to places in books they would never think of visiting in the flesh. Thousands have read *Walden* and *Life on the Mississippi*, yet how many have built a hut in the woods or rafted down a river? What is new about contemporary readers is not their preference for an indoor life, but how far indoors they are able to retreat and how long they are able to stay there. The boxes that shut us off from nature have become more perfect, more powerful, from all-electric mansions in the suburbs to glass towers in the city, from space shuttles to shopping malls. Today, the typical adult reader leaves a humming house in the morning, rides an air-conditioned car or subway to a sealed office, works eight hours under fluorescent lights, stops on the way home at night to buy frozen meat and dyed vegetables wrapped in plastic, enters the house through the garage and locks the door. Except for lawns, which are fertilized and purified to an eery shade of green, and a smoky sky, and a potted plant or two, everything this reader sees all day has been made by human beings. Only the body itself stubbornly upholds the claims of biology, and even this biological datum our reader treats with chemicals designed to improve or delay the workings of nature.

Reading this account, perhaps with a canoe strapped to the roof of your car and a compass dangling by a thong around your neck, you may scuff your boots on the floor, impatient with my dark picture. But, with all due respect, I think my campers watching a Tarzan movie in their van are more representative of the age than are the regulars on the Audubon bird count. Despite the sale of recreational gear and the traffic jams in National Parks, I believe that, on the whole, Americans today have less direct experience of nature than at any time in our history. I am not talking about occasional visits to the woods or zoo, as one might visit Grandmother in the country, but of day-to-day living contact with the organic world.

You can see this ignorance of land and landscape illustrated in the stylish fiction of our time. Read Raymond Carver's collection *What We Talk about When We Talk about Love* (1981), for example, and, aside from references to fish, deer, and geese as prey, here is the most elaborate account of nature you will find: "A big moon was laid over the mountains that went around the city. It was a white moon and covered with scars." (Read, for an instructive contrast, Thomas McGuane's *Nobody's Angel,* also published in 1981, which opens with the line, "You would have to care about the country," and over which the Montana landscape presides.) In Don DeLillo's *White Noise*—the most honored novel of 1985—the only time you are reminded that anything exists beyond the human realm is when his characters pause on the expressway to watch a sunset, and even the sunset interests them only because a release of toxic gases from a nearby plant has poisoned it into technicolor. (For a contrast to *White Noise,* read Ursula K. Le Guin's novel of the same year, *Always Coming Home,* which summons up an entire culture and cosmology governed by the most intricate and lively understanding of nature.)

Sample the novels and stories published in America today, and in the opening pages you are likely to find yourself trapped inside a room—a kitchen, perhaps, or a psychiatrist's office, a bedroom, a bar, a motel—with characters talking. When they pause in their talk, it is usually to shift into another room, where they raise their voices once again. Some might say it is inevitable that our fiction should have such an indoor cast, given that we live in an age and a place dominated by cities; inevitable that characters should display such ignorance of nature, given the shabby way we treat the environment. Of course DeLillo, Carver, Mason, and their less able imitators are reporting on our condition: surrounded by artifacts of our own making, engulfed by human racket, illiterate in the language of the cosmos. But durable art, art that matters, has never merely reproduced the superficial consciousness of an age. Cervantes did not limit himself to the platitudes of feudalism, nor Melville to Puritanism, nor Faulkner to racism, nor Garcia Marquez to nationalism and capitalism. They quarreled with the dominant ways of seeing, and in that quarreling with the actual they enlarged our vision of the possible.

However accurately it reflects the surface of our times, fiction that never looks beyond the human realm is profoundly false, and therefore pathological. No matter how urban our experience, no matter how oblivious we may be toward nature, we are nonetheless animals, two-legged sacks of meat and blood and bone dependent on the whole living planet for our survival. Our outbreathings still flow through the pores of trees, our food still grows in dirt, our bodies decay. Of course, of course: we all nod our heads in agreement. The gospel of ecology has become an *intellectual* commonplace. But it is not yet an *emotional* one. For most of us, most of the time, nature appears framed in a window or a video screen or inside the borders of a photograph. We do not feel the organic web passing through our guts. While our theories of nature have become wiser, our experience of nature has become shallower. Thus, any writer who sees the world in ecological perspective faces a hard problem: how, despite the perfection of our technological boxes, to make us feel the ache and tug of that organic web, how to *situate* the lives of characters—and therefore of readers—in nature.

How we inhabit the planet is intimately connected to how we imagine the land and its creatures. In the history of American writing about landscape, we read in brief the history of our thinking about nature and our place in the natural order. Time and again, inherited ways of seeing have given way before the powerful in-fluence of the New World landscape. If such a revolution in vision is to occur in our time, writers will have to free themselves from human enclosures, and go outside to study the green world. It may seem quaint, in the age of megalopolis, to write about wilderness or about life on farms and in small towns; it may seem escapist to write about imaginary planets where the environment shapes every human gesture; but such writing seems to me the most engaged and forward-looking we have. If we are to survive, we must look outward from the charmed circle of our own works, to the stupendous theatre where our tiny, brief play goes on.

TOKENS
OF MYSTERY

THERE IS A SAYING THAT YOU CAN TAKE THE BOY OUT of the country but you cannot take the country out of the boy. My mother, who grew up in the steel-and-concrete hive of Chicago, frequently applied this remark with a roll of her eyes to my father, who grew up on a red dirt farm in Mississippi. It was true enough in his case, and it holds true for many another country boy and girl I have known, myself included. The legacy of a rural childhood entails more than a penchant for going barefoot, say, or an itch for digging in dirt, or a taste for black-eyed peas, or a habit of speaking with lazy tongue. It also entails a relationship with the land, its rhythms and creatures. The country lingered in my father and lingers in me as a recollected intimacy with particular wild places, a memory of encounters with muskrats and mules, tornadoes and hickory trees, crickets and flooded creeks, the whole adding up to an impression of nature as grander, more intricate, and wiser than we are.

It is quite possible to grow up in the country without learning to honor nature. Drive the back roads of America, and you will see many a butchered forest, eroded field, and poisoned creek, many a trash dump, many a tattered animal shot up for the sheer joy of killing, all the handiwork of country people. In fact, the history of rural America has been largely one of slash and plunder. Familiarity with a landscape may breed no more than contempt, if our eyes have been trained to see contemptuously, or it may breed devotion, if we have learned to see reverently. In the book of Job, the beleaguered man proclaims that all creatures rest in the hand of God:

> But ask the beasts, and they will teach you;
>   the birds of the air, and they will tell you;
> or the plants of the earth, and they will teach you;
>   and the fish of the sea will declare to you.

The key word here is *ask*. What the birds and beasts and countryside teach us depends on the questions we pose. A person wielding a fifty-ton digger in search of coal will learn quite different lessons from one who wields a pair of binoculars in search of warblers. Job assumed that anybody who listened to the creation would hear the whisper of the creator. But generally we hear what our ears have been prepared for, and if we do not go seeking divinity we are not likely to find it. In the long run and in a blunt manner, nature has its own say: species that poison or exhaust their habitat die out. But in the short run, nature does not declare how we should approach it; that lesson we learn from culture.

For me as a child, "culture" meant first of all my parents, and then a few neighbors, then books and teachers, and only much later, when I was largely set in my ways, photographs and paintings and films. Plucking a pheasant, sawing down a tree, walking through a woods, planting beans, gathering blackberries, watching the moon, my parents acted out of a joyous, wondering regard for nature. To my mother, the budding of pussy willows or the reddening of maples announced the eras of our lives with more authority than anything the calendar or newspaper had to say. To my father, the pawprints of a raccoon in the mud beside a creek, or the persistent flowing of the creek itself, were tokens of an inexhaustible mystery. I learned from my parents a thousand natural facts, but above all I learned how to stand on the earth, how to address the creation, and how to listen.

Because of their example, I was drawn to those of our Ohio neighbors who shared this regard for nature— the elderly Swedish couple who let me help with maple sugaring, the carpenter who brooded on the grain in wood, the biology teacher who lived in a wild meadow (sight of her musing among the waist-high flowers left a deeper impression on me than any lecture or textbook), the dairy farmers, horse trainers, muskrat trappers, hunters of fossils, feeders of birds. Their example in turn prepared me to read with gusto about Mark Twain's Mississippi River, Thoreau's Walden Pond, Black Elk's High

Plains, Annie Dillard's Roanoke Valley, Wendell Berry's Kentucky, Barry Lopez's Arctic, and the many other intimate landscapes in our literature. I moved easily from literary visions of nature to visions inspired by science in the pages of Rachel Carson, Loren Eiseley, Lewis Thomas, and Stephen Jay Gould. Reading prepared me to relish the paintings of Thomas Cole and George Inness, the photographs of Ansel Adams, the films of Jacques Cousteau, the music and ceremonies of Native Americans.

Thus begun on a path of ardent inquiry about the cosmos, I hope to make new discoveries so long as I live. Needless to say, I haven't always lived up to these models for dwelling in nature—I close myself inside human shells, I stop my ears and blinker my eyes, I squander the fruits of the earth—and yet, inscribed with those models in childhood, I always know when I have fallen away.

Meanwhile, just down the road from us lived a man and woman who whipped their horses, kicked their dogs, ruined their soil, and threw trash out the back door. Their children grew up doing likewise. Surrounded by the same landscape, the same beasts and weather as our family, these neighbors inhabited a radically different "nature" from the one we knew. Their conversation with the earth was carried on in a language foreign to the one I learned in my own household. You can grow up in the country and remain blissfully ignorant of nature, and you can behave as callously toward the earth as any city slicker. But still, love the land or hate it, attune yourself to its rhythms or mine it for dollars, the one thing you cannot do, having grown up in the country, is ignore it.

You know in your bones that nature surrounds and sustains every least thing we do.

I AM NEVER MORE AWARE of being an overgrown backwoods boy than when I sojourn in a city. Recently transplanted for a year from a small Indiana town, where deer still occasionally graze in backyards, to Boston, where the yards have been paved and the deer pose on billboards, I found myself wondering how children in cities experience nature. When these children grow up, and some of them become the potentates who decide how we should occupy the planet, what images of nature will govern their decisions? For me this was a question of private as well as public consequence, because my nine-year-old son and fourteen-year-old daughter were sharing Boston with me. Having them on hand meant I could snoop on youth without going far afield. I emerged from months of snooping with a gloomy opinion of cities as places for learning about nature, but with an increased respect for the imagination, resourcefulness, and curiosity of children.

Suppose you are a child taking a walk in downtown Boston. What flickers of wildness do you see amid the skyscrapers, glassy shops, condominiums, and parking lots? Well, you see dogs on leashes, sickly trees and shrubs (not quite on leashes, but planted in boxes and surrounded by fences to protect them from human assault), an occasional strip of grass that is kept alive by infusions of chemicals, cut flowers for sale on street corners, pigeons roosting on windowsills, rats nosing in alleys. If you make your way to that fabled green space, the Public Garden, which is entirely hemmed in by a palisade of buildings, you will discover a concrete pond aswim with pinioned ducks (except after frost, when authorities drain the pool to avoid law suits), a row of elms bearing name tags, a cemetery, a baseball diamond, two subway stops, a six-lane boulevard, an expanse of trampled lawn planted with statues, and signs everywhere announcing what is forbidden. Since the avenues yield no glimpses of robust or unfettered nature, you might seek out water. But like most rivers that have the ill fortune to wind through cities, the Charles is a docile and filthy gutter, girded by walls, laced with bridges, hemmed in by highways, and slick with oil. The river's poisons collect in the harbor, which has become a gray desert encircled by shipyards, airport, docks, and high-rise apartments.

In this great outdoors of Boston, the only remnants of nature, aside from rats, that look as though they might survive without our ministrations are the sun and sky glimpsed overhead between glass towers. If you are bold enough to walk abroad at night, you will search for the stars in vain through the glare of streetlights. The breeze is laden with diesel fumes and the rumble of engines. By going indoors—into a shopper's nirvana such as Copley Place, for example, or a corporate stronghold such as the Prudential building—you can escape even the sky and its weathers, withdraw from seasons and the vagaries of sunlight. In grocery stores, cows show up sliced and weighed into red hunks, chickens go featherless in Styrofoam tubs, wheat disappears along with a dose of additives into gaudy packages, even apples and oranges wear a camouflage of dye. Day or night, indoors or out, nature in the city appears as a slavish power, rather puny and contemptible, supplying us with decoration, amusement, or food, always framed by our purposes, summoned or banished according to our whims.

Of course, like all reasonably affluent cities that take the burdens of enlightenment seriously, Boston provides its children with places to confront nature, as it were, in the flesh. Chief among these are the zoo, where morose animals pace in cages; the aquarium, where fish circle in tanks; the arboretum, where trees that never rub limbs in the wild grow side by side and bear identifying labels; and the science museum, where the universe comes packaged in mind-sized dollops, usually jazzed up with electronics.

Fitted with a pair of child's eyes, let us pay a visit to the New England Aquarium. Outside, you watch three seals cruise in a small white pool shaped like a rhomboid. Two beats of the rear flippers carry them from end to end. You admire their grace, but soon realize that you have seen every move they are likely to make in such a cramped, sterile space. Inside the building, on the ground floor, you hang over the rail of a larger pool to observe a colony of jackass penguins, some of them zipping through the green shallows, some teetering across the fiberglass islands. Just when you are beginning to feel a sense of how these dapper birds might carry on in their own realm, a diver splashes into the pool. From plastic buckets he doles out fish to the assembled penguins, noting on a clipboard the dietary selection for each bird. Meanwhile, from the balcony overhead, a technician lowers a thermometer on a wire above the head of each penguin in turn and records the temperatures on yet another clipboard. If you are like my son, you find the electronics and wet suits more impressive than these birds that must be fed like babies. If you are like my daughter, you are distracted by the other kids who shoulder you aside for a view of the proceedings.

From the ground floor you climb a spiral ramp, passing tank after tank in which sea creatures browse or snooze in tiny simulated habitats—inky murk for the ocean depths, crashing surf for the coastal shallows, weedy thickets and algal pools. These exhibits go some way toward showing us nature in its own terms, as a web of life, a domain of nonhuman forces. And yet these miniature habitats with their listless swimmers are still merely pictures framed and labeled by the masters; they are images viewed, like those on television, through windows of glass.

From the top floor you gaze down into a huge cylindrical tank, which houses a four-story fiberglass replica of a coral reef and several hundred species of fish. The size of it, the painted reef, the mixture of species all give some feel for the larger patterns of the sea. And yet immediately a naturalist begins lecturing while a diver descends to feed the sharks. "You think they'll bite him?" the children ask, their minds bearing Hollywood images of underwater killers, nature measured on a scale of menace. By means of another ramp you spiral down along the circumference of this tank, stopping to press your nose through a wavery thickness of glass against the snout of a moray eel. That is communion of a sort. Downstairs, a film about the artificial reef celebrates the imitation more than the ocean's original, dwelling on the ingenuity of the builders, the strength of the walls, the weight of glass and steel, thereby confirming your sense that nature is fortunate indeed to have been packaged by such clever artisans.

A bell rings, calling you to the eleven o'clock water show. You rush to the auditorium, squeeze into a seat, then watch as a trainer puts a seal and three dolphins through their paces. The trainer is an earnest woman, who explains how intelligent these animals are, how cantankerous, how creative, but all you see are dolphins jumping through hoops and retrieving rubber toys, a seal balancing a ball on its nose and smacking its flippers at jokes, all you hear are the synchronized splashes, the whistles and grunts of programmed clowns.

Visit the zoo in Franklin Park—or any zoo, even the most spacious and ecologically minded—and you find nature parceled out into showy fragments, a nature demeaned and dominated by our constructions. Thickets of bamboo and simulated watering holes cannot disguise the elementary fact that a zoo is a prison. The animals are captives, hauled to this place for our edification or entertainment. No matter how ferocious they may look, they are wholly dependent on our care. A bear squatting on its haunches, a tiger lounging with half-lidded eyes, a bald eagle hunched on a limb are like refugees who tell us less about their homeland, their native way of being, than about our power. In the zoo they exist without purposes of their own, cut off from their true place on earth and from the cycles demanded by their flesh.

Visit the Museum of Science, a lively playhouse aimed at luring children into a reasoned study of the cosmos, and again you find nature whittled down to fragments. Most of the exhibits have to do, not with nature, but with our inventions—satellites, steam engines, airplanes, computers, telephones, lasers, robots, cars, Van de Graaff generators—a display of human power that merely echoes the lessons of the city. As though to compensate, a number of the creaturely exhibits are gigantic—a fullscale model of Tyrannosaurus rex, a grasshopper the size of a delivery van, an immense brain (ours, of course, thereby reminding us where the center of the cosmos lies). But no matter how large, the beasts themselves are manifestly artificial, further proofs of our ingenuity. "Wow," cry the children, "how did they make *that?*" The nearest you come to nature's own products is in the hall of dioramas, where stuffed animals, encased in glass, pose in habitat groups against painted backdrops. How long will you stand before these dusty, silent, rigid carcasses, while, from elsewhere in the museum, our own handiworks beckon with luminous colors, bright lights, synthetic voices, and flashy movements?

On a wall of the museum there is a quotation from Aristotle: "The search for the Truth is in one way hard and in another easy—for it is evident that no one of us can ever master it fully, nor miss it wholly. Each one of us adds a little to our knowledge of nature and from all the facts assembled arises a certain grandeur." Worthy sentiments; yet the facts assembled in the museum, like the bits of nature scattered through the city, point to no grandeur except our own.

So long as we meet nature in fragments and in human containers, we cannot see it truly. Even when science is called in to explain what we are beholding, it comes to seem, not so much a way of reading the cosmos, as an instrument of power. Without wishing to deny the educational zeal of those who run the museum, the zoo, the aquarium, or the other city arenas for the display of nature, I want to emphasize how belittling, how dangerously one-sided are the impressions these arenas create. Sight of stuffed antelopes, trees behind fences, gorillas behind bars, penguins in tanks, and flowers in pots will more likely inspire contempt than awe. Snared in our inventions, wearing our labels, the plants and animals stand mute. In such places, the loudest voice we hear is our own.

NONE OF THE FOREGOING is meant as a diatribe against Boston in particular—a place I delight in—nor against cities in general, but rather as a sober account of the peculiar, even pathological image of nature the city provides. Recognizing how distorted this image is, we should feel the necessity of making available to our children a wiser and healthier one. Although my view of cities as places for learning about nature is gloomy, my view of children as learners is hopeful. Against all odds, many an urban child acquires a sense of the dignity, integrity, and majestic self-sufficiency of nature. How does this come about? For the beginnings of an answer, let me describe a conversation with my son Jesse.

One day that winter in Boston he and I set out for the library on foot. Whenever Jesse steps outdoors, all his senses come alert. Before we had even crossed the street, he squatted down to examine a slab of ice in the gutter. The slab had broken in two, and the pieces, gliding on their own meltwater, had slipped a hand's width apart. After a moment of scrutiny, tracing the ice with a finger, he observed, "These are like the continents drifting on molten rock."

This led us to discuss the geological theory of plate tectonics, about which we had seen a documentary on television. According to the theory, earthquakes are caused by the friction of adjoining plates as they rub against one another. We tried this out on the ice, shoving the two pieces together until their edges grated, and were rewarded by the feel of tremors passing up through our gloved hands. Continuing our walk to the library, we then recalled what a friend of the family, a seismologist, had told us concerning his study of earthquakes in the Soviet Union, and what that study revealed about the structure of the earth.

"I read in school," Jesse told me excitedly, "how Chinese scientists have discovered a kind of fish that can feel when earthquakes are coming, even before machines can."

In reply, I told how one time John James Audubon was riding near the Ohio River, when his usually obedient horse stopped dead in its tracks and spread its legs as though to keep from tumbling over. What in blazes? Audubon thought. Neither word nor whip could make the horse budge—and a good thing, too, for several minutes later the ground buckled and the trees rocked from the New Madrid earthquake.

"You know," Jesse mused, "lots of animals have keener senses than we do. Like the way coon dogs can smell, and the way birds can travel using landmarks and stars and the earth's magnetism."

He had learned of coon dogs from a grandfather's stories, of celestial navigation from a visit to a whaling museum, of migration from magazines and from our habit of watching, every spring and fall, for the unerring movements of ducks and geese overhead. We then talked about the night vision of owls and the daylight vision of ospreys, birds we had met on our camping trips.

"If I could see like an eagle," said Jesse, "I'd be able to spot tiny things like field mice from way high up. But would I be able to see in color?"

Since that question stumped me, and since by then we had reached the library, we decided to look it up. None of the books gave a clear-cut answer, but one of them did say that birds of prey owe their acute vision to the dense packing of rods and cones in their retinas. From the dictionary we then learned that rods are sensitive to dim light, cones to bright light and colors. So we had our answer, and in our excitement gave one another a boisterous high-five hand slap that provoked a glower from the librarian.

In skimming the encyclopedia articles, Jesse had noticed that birds have a rapid heartbeat. How fast was his own? We timed his pulse: eighty beats per minute. How fast was mine? Fifty-five. How come his was faster? I told him it was partly because of our relative size—small bodies lose heat more quickly than large ones—and partly because children have a higher rate of metabolism than adults. What's metabolism? Jesse wanted to know. So we talked about how cells turn food into energy and tissue.

"Like we get energy from milk," said Jesse, "and the cow gets energy from grass, and the grass gets energy from the sun. I bet if you go back far enough, you can track every kind of food to the sun."

By now, our rucksacks filled with a new supply of books, we were moseying toward home. On the way, Jesse kept up his flurry of questions and speculations. Could humans live by eating grass? Why doesn't grass use up the soil and wear it out? How much grass would a big wild critter like a buffalo have to eat every day to stay alive? Smoke rising from a chimney then set him talking about wind patterns, acid rain, forests. If bad chemicals fall on the grass—lead, say, from diesel trucks—and cattle graze on it, and we eat the cattle in our hamburgers, the poison winds up in us, right?

And so, within the space of an hour, driven forward by Jesse's curiosity, we moved from a broken slab of ice to the geology of earth, from earthquakes to eagles, from the anatomy of eyes to the biology of food chains. No telling where we might have gone next. Out front of our place one of Jesse's buddies led him off to play street hockey.

Such conversations do not happen every day, but they happen frequently enough to persuade me that Jesse is persistently, eagerly building a model of nature, one that will make sense of the full variety of his experience. As that experience enlarges, so he continually revises his model. In this one conversation he drew from books, magazines, school, radio, and television (public radio and public television: to seek knowledge of nature on the commercial channels is like searching for a moose in a parking lot); he drew from his memories of camping trips, gardening, hikes in the woods, seaside rambles, mealtime conversations, family stories, visits to museums, talks with adult friends (a geologist, a physician, a bird-watcher, a farmer), drew from all of these sources in an attempt to see nature whole. He needed every scrap of this experience and would have used anything else his nine years might have provided.

Jesse shares with all children this voracious hunger to make sense of things, but his *way* of making sense bears the stamp of his upbringing. Having spent most of his life in a house with a wildflower garden in the backyard, in a town surrounded by forests and creeks, having known farmers and stone quarriers and biologists, and having spent many hours with his family tramping through the countryside, he knows without being told that nature is our ultimate home. What the city has to say about nature—in museums, zoos, parks—he understands in light of what he has already learned from the country. Watching California gray whales migrate along the Pacific coast prepared him to view without condescension the dolphins that jump through hoops; because he has watched pileated woodpeckers graze on dead trees and white-tailed deer cross a meadow like ripples of pure energy, he knows that beasts in cages are lords in exile.

IN THOREAU'S EXULTANT PHRASE from *Walden*, "We need to witness our own limits transgressed, and some life pasturing freely where we never wander." This is all the more crucial for urban children, who live in a maze of human invention. If a child is to have an expansive and respectful vision of nature, there is no substitute for direct encounters with wildness. This means passing unprogrammed days and weeks in the mountains, the woods, the fields, beside rivers and oceans, territories where plants and beasts are the natives and we are the visitors. Ideally, children should witness "life pasturing freely" in the company of adults who are intimately aware of nature's pulse and pattern. As parents, we can assure our children of such company, not by turning them over to experts, but by cultivating this awareness in ourselves.

My own parents never *told* me how I should feel about nature; they communicated their own deep regard for that larger order by their manner of living. On hearing the call of geese, my father would drop whatever he was doing and rush outside. On visiting a new place, he would scoop up a handful of dirt to get the feel of it, the smell and taste of it. When I was small enough to ride in his arms, during thunderstorms he would bundle me in a blanket and carry me onto the porch and hold me against his chest while we listened to the rain sizzle down. My mother would tramp across a bog to admire a lady's slipper or a toad. When I first read Dylan Thomas's fierce lines,

> The force that through the green fuse drives the flower
> Drives my green age; that blasts the roots of trees
> Is my destroyer,

it was a truth I had already learned from her. She was alive to designs everywhere—in the whorls of her palm and the spirals of a chambered nautilus, in the crystals of milky quartz, the carapace of a snapping turtle, the flukes of a mushroom, the whiskers of a mouse. Neither of my parents was a scientist, but they were both eager to learn everything science could tell them about the workings of the world.

Fashioning a vision of nature is one of the urgent enterprises of childhood. I believe that Jesse's curiosity, his desire to understand and feel at home on the earth, is typical of young children. The child inhabits a compact wilderness called the body, with which he or she reaches out to all other living things. Look at a child, and you see an organism perfectly equipped for investigating the world—wide-awake eyes, quick brain, avid mouth, irrepressible hands. Nothing is lost on children, so long as it brings news from previously unknown regions. Their questions not only probe the universe; they probe us. How much do we understand of the workings of the cosmos and of our place within it? Where we are ignorant, do we know (or care) how to search for answers? Daily companionship with a questioning child is a reminder of what intelligence is *for*—not, ultimately, for dominion, but for communion. Children are transcendentalists by instinct, reading in the humblest natural fact a sign of some greater pattern. Unlike a grown-up—who might often with more accuracy be called a grown-rigid—children will only settle for a cramped, belittling, domineering view of nature if that is all we offer them. So let us offer them tokens of the creation, that elegant wildness, that encompassing order which calls for our full powers of understanding and, when mind has stretched as far as it will go, for love.

SECRETS

OF THE

UNIVERSE

I HAVE BEEN BRUSHING UP ON PHYSICS LATELY, THE WAY travelers preparing for a journey will brush up on a foreign language they once spoke with ease. There was a time in high school and college when I *thought* in physics. I doodled formulas on cafeteria napkins. I traced parabolas in the flight of baseballs. While drifting off to sleep I would memorize atomic weights from a periodic table of the elements that was pasted to the wall beside my bed. Teeter-totters in playgrounds made me think of problems in torque, Ferris wheels spoke to me of angular momentum, a glimpse of legs seemingly bent by the water of a swimming pool illustrated the index of refraction.

Even in my airiest moments as a physicist, when the sight of a suicide leaping from a roof might have led me to calculate the speed he would be going when he hit the sidewalk, there were limits to my obsession. If the legs in the swimming pool belonged to a girl of the right age and shape, my first thoughts would have nothing to do with refraction. If the girl's hair happened to be a tempting color, only after I imagined stroking it would I think about the frequency of reflected light.

One day in science class, the teacher made a dozen of us form a ring by holding hands, and then shot a mild charge of electricity through our joined fingers. As it happened, I took my place in the ring between two girls I'd set my heart on, so when the jolt of electricity slammed through, instead of reflecting on the conductivity of flesh as the teacher meant for us to do, I could think of nothing but those two fidgety, mouse-quick hands squirming in mine. The first time I ran across W. B. Yeats's feisty little poem that opens with the lines

> How can I, that girl standing there,
> My attention fix
> On Roman or on Russian
> Or on Spanish politics?

in place of *politics* I read *physics*, which made perfect sense to me, although it spoiled the rhythm.

Aside from sex, very little distracted me from physics in those days. While my schoolmates customized Chevrolets or fattened calves, I mixed gunpowder in the basement and launched rockets from the barn lot next to our pigpen. (I used the pigpen as a blockhouse, running ignition wires out between the stout oak planks and watching the launch through a knothole. The pigs themselves had long since gone the way of tenderloin and bacon.) My steady orders for sulphur, saltpeter, and powdered zinc greatly puzzled the local druggist; the neighborhood machinist, who specialized in making parts for tractors, was driven to distraction by my requests for combustion chambers fashioned from chrome-molybdenum alloys. My authority in these matters was the *Rocket Manual for Amateurs,* where I read that, "There is no essential difference between a rocket and a bomb, except that the rocket has a hole in one end (and this hole can become blocked)." In case of an untimely explosion, the manual advised in capital letters, STOP THE BLEEDING, PROTECT THE WOUND, PREVENT OR TREAT SHOCK. When mixing fuels the amateur rocketeer was supposed to wear a heavy rubber apron, asbestos gloves, face shield, goggles, and gas mask. Since I did not own any of these items, and since I knew that a request to buy such disaster gear would have alarmed my already nervous parents, I made do with work gloves and a welder's mask. One evening a spark from a dropped screwdriver set off a pan of black powder I was mixing in the basement, and the acrid smoke rising through the floor registers into the living room set off my parents, who put a swift end to my career as a rocketeer.

Physics could not shake me that easily, however. During summers in high school I built houses, and the framework of studs and joists became for me a web of vectors. For a period of several weeks, while I carried two-by-fours and hammered sixteen-penny nails, I thought I had discovered a way to improve on Einstein's general theory of relativity. (This was at roughly the same age when I thought I could give Willy Mays a few tips about catching fly balls.) With a carpenter's pencil I wrote my notions on a sheet of plywood that was later used for decking on the roof. To this day, unless the place burned down or ascended to heaven in a tornado, there is a house in Ohio with my refinements on relativity hidden beneath the shingles. Never mind that I did not understand the first thing about Einstein's formulas; I was convinced that I had pried loose a new secret from the universe. After those few heady weeks, I explained my discovery to a teacher, who straightened me out in five minutes.

DURING SUMMERS IN COLLEGE I drove a forklift on the graveyard shift in a Louisiana factory. While I sat on the greasy seat waiting for loaders to fill the next pallet, I worked calculus problems on the backs of shipping tickets. The other drivers—mostly Cajuns, with names like Goux and Le Doux, Dreaux and Thibideaux—would sometimes park their forklifts beside mine to watch me scrawl numbers and symbols. What I wrote was the deepest mystery to them, hieroglyphics from another planet; yet to me it was the most lucid and coherent of games. Around me the factory clanked and fumed, machines broke down, men lost fingers and tempers; but on the pale green field of my shipping ticket everything was tidy, clear, governed by unambiguous rules. While our forklifts idled beneath us, the Cajun drivers would tell me about their divorces, shoot-outs with in-laws, debts, doubts, and all the puzzles that flesh is heir to, and I would feel that, beside their baffling lives, my calculations were childishly simple.

In those years, when my own shifting emotions swept through me like rival street gangs, when the world of adulthood looked murkier and more dangerous than the New York subway, I found deep comfort in the orderliness and clarity of physics. Even the launching of crude rockets from a pigpen enabled me to taste the intoxicating sweetness that Robert Oppenheimer spoke about during his trial: "When you see something that is technically sweet, you go ahead and do it and you argue about what to do about it only after you have had your technical success. That is the way it was with the atomic bomb." In the rarefied world of mathematics, most problems could be solved; in the gritty world outside, solutions came hard. I could have told you how fast the suicide was traveling when he smacked the sidewalk, but I could not have told you why he jumped. I understood why free electrons flowed through a circle of joined hands, but not why a girl's fingers against my palm set my heart racing.

To suggest how long ago this was, when I last spoke physics as my natural tongue I did my calculating on a slide rule. I still keep it in a drawer of my desk, ready for mathematical emergencies, a lemon-yellow Pickett slide rule made of aluminum, with a leather-covered hardshell case. I had to load hay all one sticky August to pay for it. On the case there is a loop I used for attaching it to my belt, like a short sword. Most girls did not feel easy talking with boys who wore slide rules, so it soon became a concealed weapon. Then one summer I met a girl who not only carried a Pickett in her purse, but who understood logarithms and differential equations; so as soon as I graduated from college I married her.

My devotion to the girl proved more durable than my devotion to physics. Eventually I discovered that my mind is by nature messy rather than precise; it sprawls and leaps instead of boring straight holes. When this slovenly mind seizes on a pattern, however, it clings stubbornly. If I play too much chess, or do too much electrical wiring, or work too many algebra problems, the patterns of chessboard or wires or equations will circle through me relentlessly. The higher I climbed into the abstractions of physics, the harder it was for me to breathe, the more keenly I missed the racket and smells and dizzying sights of the everyday world. I also discovered that several of my teachers were funded by the Pentagon, and I had grim visions of traveling each year to Washington, slide rule in hand, blueprints for weapons rolled beneath my arm, to ask the generals for money. It troubled me to realize that the pure ideas of physics, after passing through the hands of powermongers, often killed people. (When I read in Auden's elegy for Yeats that "poetry makes nothing happen," I envied poets. I have since realized that deadly ideas also crop up in sonnets and speeches and Bibles and philosophical tracts.) So in my final year of college I decided to switch from the study of physics to a field that was its polar opposite—muddled, ambiguous, invisible to politicians and investors, without any prospect of altering the world let alone of killing people—and thus I wound up in literature. Nothing has been clear for me since.

Feeling nostalgic for order lately, I have been working my way through *Physics Made Simple*. In the years since I spoke physics with ease, it seems that *I* have been made simple. Still, I plug away at the story problems, using, in place of my elegant Pickett slide rule, a Texas Instruments scientific calculator. If I had owned such a magical black box when I was in college—if such boxes had even existed—I might have stayed in physics, and would now be juggling formulas for a living instead of stringing together these lumps of language. One morning recently, stumped by a problem in writing, I took up a problem in thermodynamics. I had the slide rule out, toying with it, when my son puttered in, rubbing his eyes from sleep. "Hey," he said, perking up at sight of the shiny gadget, "what's *that*?" I told him it was a calculator dating from the time before the invention of computer chips. He knew that my own childhood had fallen somewhere between the building of the pyramids and the building of moon rockets, so he was prepared for my relics from antiquity. "That's cool," he said. "How does it work?" I showed him, and we spent the hour before breakfast figuring batting averages for the Cincinnati Reds.

HAVING REVIVED THE OLD LANGUAGE of physics in my rusty brain, once again I see equations everywhere. At dusk on the Fourth of July, for instance, while a crowd of neighbors nibbling picnic leftovers milled about in front of our house and waited for the evening fireworks, a friend and I launched a homemade hot-air balloon, and this humble event set me thinking about the ideal gas law, buoyancy, acceleration due to gravity, wind vectors, Bernoulli's principle, and other bits of elementary physics. In preparation for the launch, my friend Malcolm rolled from the driveway his daughter's red wagon, which held a two-gallon potato chip can, which held a charcoal fire. Wearing leather-palmed gloves, he rigged over this burner a makeshift hood of tin with a section of stovepipe for a chimney. This contraption did not inspire confidence in the crowd. Grown-ups and kids alike buzzed with skepticism. When I spread out the legs of my stepladder in the middle of the street beside the wagon, then climbed to the topmost rung with the gaudy paper balloon folded in pleats over my shoulder, the skeptical buzz grew as harsh as locust song.

Malcolm and I had made the balloon by cutting and gluing together swatches of striped, clown-colored tissue paper—orange and green and pink and blue—all crinkly and light, like starched pajamas. Once inflated, it would resemble a six-foot-high pear turned upside down. At least that is how we hoped it would look, how the design we had sketched on a leaf of notebook paper said it should look. At the moment, draped in folds over my shoulder, it might have been a collapsed awning. I did not blame the onlookers for scoffing.

While I teetered on the highest rung of the ladder—the one labeled: DANGER, DO NOT STAND ON OR ABOVE THIS STEP, YOU CAN LOSE YOUR BALANCE—and held the balloon by its topknot, Malcolm fitted the neck down over the stovepipe. Within seconds the hot air rising from the chimney began to swell the balloon, which crackled as it unfolded, the papery sounds striking the onlookers dumb with amazement. All right, I imagined them thinking, you guys can puff up a balloon with a charcoal fire, but you'll never make it *fly.*

Soon, from my perch on the ladder, instead of holding the balloon up I was holding it *down.* It bobbed under my hand, buoyant, like a gigantic beach ball floating in water. Beneath my hands the paper felt warm, almost hot, about the temperature of clothes fresh from the dryer. Down below, Malcolm kept saying, "What do you think? Is it ready?" He was so giddy, fidgeting beside the red wagon, I thought he might lift off before the balloon.

The great bulging sack swayed beneath my hands, nervous, alive, and I remembered stroking the bellies of horses. From the crowd, children pressed inward to form a tight whispery ring around the base of the ladder. "When's it going to fly?" one of them cried.

"How about now?" Malcolm said.

"Now!" I agreed. And we both let go.

The balloon shivered free of our hands and rose slowly toward the gap of sky between the overhanging trees. The crowd cheered. Stately, florid as a tropical fish, the balloon climbed up past the elms and suddenly caught the late dusky sunlight, which set the bright colors ablaze. Understanding the physical reasons for the flight did not keep me from watching slackjawed and joyful as the balloon drifted to the north over trees and chimneys. My jaw stiffened as our creation sailed out of sight, whereupon I jumped on my bicycle and gave chase, thinking as I pedaled northward that the universe is after all a generous place for allowing us to coax so much beauty from a sack of hot air.

WITHOUT ANY HELP FROM US—without benefit of charcoal burners or red wagons or tissue paper—the universe achieves a good measure of drama through the periodic visits of that great iceball named Halley's Comet. The return of the comet a few years ago stirred up a commotion in my neighborhood. In the checkout lines at grocery stores and beside gas pumps I would hear folks asking one another breathlessly, "Have you seen it? What's it look like?" Newspapers printed maps to guide the astronomically ignorant to a clear view of this marvel. Television carried interviews with oldsters who remembered having seen the comet last time around. Business in binoculars and telescopes boomed. I didn't see any gas masks for sale locally, perhaps because midwesterners are too familiar with lightning and tornadoes to worry about poisonous vapors in the tails of comets. But I did see T-shirts emblazoned with images of the comet, and rubber balls with streamers designed for playing comet-catch, and comet slush-cones at the ice cream shops, and other gewgaws aimed at cashing in on the return of Mr. Halley's wonder.

Still, it was a welcome visit. Behind the hoopla, the comet's return was a reminder that we are tiny, transient creatures in a very large and orderly house. Just such an intimation of the size, intricacy, and elegance of the cosmos had lured me as a boy to the study of science, and lures me still. Friedrich Schiller spoke for many literary types when he accused science of having brought about the "disenchantment of the world." He didn't speak for me. Although I am no more than a casual tourist in the country of physics, what I find there is consistently enchanting. Just the other day I read that certain physicists, puzzling over why the sun seems to produce too few neutrinos and why the universe appears to be missing 90 percent of the matter predicted by current theories, have dreamed up new entities called WIMPs—weakly interacting massive particles—to make up the difference. It is rather as if your bank statement showed you deeply in debt, and you balanced your checkbook by attributing the deficit to withdrawals by ghosts. Physicists love to propose new particles or planets or galaxies to make their equations work out; and then, as often as not, when they go looking for their inventions they find them. Washing dishes one of these mornings I will hear over the radio that some laboratory has cornered a WIMP and taken its picture. I wonder sometimes if nature, watching us grope for understanding, cooks up new phenomena to fit our theories. It would be a tiring job for nature—unless, as seems possible, the chief business of the universe is play.